Behind the Ivy Walls

Hal English

BLACK ROSE
writing™

ISBN: 978-1-61296-363-1

PUBLISHED BY BLACK ROSE WRITING

www.blackrosewriting.com

Printed in the United States of America

Behind the Ivy Walls is printed in Gentium Book Basic

This book is dedicated to the 1.6 million homeless children in America.

Dare to believe in yourself and learn to thrive because you absolutely matter!

Behind the Ivy Walls

PROLOGUE

This heartbreaking story is based on a true account of one child's journey through a life where nothing is as it seems, nor makes any sense. The reader follows young Harold as he recounts his amazing and often shocking adventures of survival.

There were six children in the family and a renowned but somewhat fanatical psychiatrist for a father. Harold was the chosen one of the six children ... chosen for abuse.

The Lord of the Manor, Dr. Harrison Force English, was a skillfully educated professional, trained at doling out mental as well as physical pain. He expertly used his words as weapons and he knew just what to say and just when to say it to scar a child as hurtfully as possible. Dr. English supervised patients at the Trenton State Psychiatric Hospital, where it was shockingly revealed that psychiatric patients were mistreated right up until their deaths, some even after.

As a teenager Harold began trying to make sense of his life after his father died a slow and horrible death. The boy left home to avoid being a burden on his mother and the other children and also out of fear and to escape the haunting memories of abuse. With no place to go, he became homeless and struggled to stay alive.

Harold's sometimes tragic but always compelling journey includes the heartrending story of his first two real friends in life, Jap and Freddy, both wonderful and promising young boys whom met early and tragic ends.

When accidentally discovering that he was secretly adopted he begins an eighteen-year journey to find his biological father and family. Each chapter of this story uncovers a new revelation about Harold's dark family secrets uncovered one by one. It reveals a family history deliberately buried—baggage that the English family never wanted nor could have exposed to the outside world.

Behind the Ivy Walls is based on true accounts of adultery, blackmail, bigamy, attempted murder, and finally an almost unimaginable act of revenge enacted by Dr. Harrison Force English and a final bombshell delivered with the force of a Howitzer cannon by his mother.

CHAPTER ONE

ENGLISH MANOR

Life inside those stunning ivy-covered walls wasn't as it may have seemed to the neighborhood folks living on the outside. Growing up inside the English Manor, it felt, at least to this little boy, that the world was a frigid and heartless place. That's all I knew of life, what went on inside those walls.

The entire exterior of the manor was blanketed with the climbing woody stems and green-and-white leaves. My small and sheltered world—along with my nightmares—was smothered in them.

To most people in Trenton, New Jersey, innocent-looking ivy growing up the side of a stone English Tudor house was a symbol of a quiet, tranquil peace and prosperity. Only the rich had homes made from the imported stone that allowed the ivy to cling and thrive.

Ivy was a silencer, buffering the noise of the people and traffic outside for the occupants who lived inside the house. To me, it was the opposite. The ivy muffled the constant weeping and grief that was occurring every day inside the mansion, making it inaudible to the people outside.

In my subconscious, that ivy is everywhere, clinging and choking my memories, creeping and crawling unchecked and out of control all around my recollections of my childhood. First there was the ivy on the English Manor, then the ivy covering the Trenton Psychiatric Hospital, and finally the ivy attached to the Saint Michael's Orphanage. The ivy wrapped itself around my young mind and became a symbol of entrapment. It was a twisted anguish, and I dreamed of one day disentangling myself and cutting myself free.

I vividly remember that the stone on our house was always cool to the touch, even in the summer heat. I wondered if the chilly temperature of the rock contributed to the cold emotional atmosphere inside the manor.

Even today, I have an aversion to ivy; it haunts my recollections and has a recurring role in my nightmares. How could such an innocent plant be such a daunting nemesis?

In later years, when people discovered that I lived at the English Manor as a boy, they would tell me that when they passed by the house they tried to envision what a wonderful life the children living there must have. They imagined that growing up in such a remarkable dwelling was something special, the ultimate life. Little did they know, for me the house was the proverbial gilded cage in which I was hopelessly and completely trapped.

People say a house is not a home without a heart and soul. To me our house had no heart, but it did have quite a few souls—some lost souls.

It appears that I had it all. My father was a wealthy and renowned doctor, and my mother was a strikingly attractive woman with a deep German accent that drove men wild.

Trenton, at the time, was a city of 80,000 people, mostly blue collar. The city was predominantly known in history as the place where General George Washington crossed the Delaware River on Christmas day to fight and defeat the British Army. The bloody Battle of Trenton in 1776 became the turning point of the American Revolution.

In the 1950s and 1960s, while I was growing up, Trenton was an industrial marvel. Just about anything and everything one could possibly need was built in the city. It was there that John A. Roebling manufactured wire rope for both the Brooklyn and Golden Gate bridges as well as for other famous landmarks around the world.

Trenton's nickname in those days was "the Staffordshire of America," because it was the pottery capital of the United States.

To this day, a world famous truss bridge in Trenton spans the Delaware River separating New Jersey and Pennsylvania. The bridge was built in the early 1800s and was emblazoned in 1935 with huge illuminated letters boldly proclaiming, "Trenton Makes the World Takes." That sign and slogan are still in use today, though it's hard to imagine why. Today the city is littered with abandoned buildings from its industrial glory days, and it is hard to find a factory manufacturing anything in the metropolis.

I was the third of six children in my family. My father, a renowned psychiatrist, thoroughly relished the ego trip of being a blueblood. The English family's ancestors had come to America on the Mayflower with the Pilgrims, and my father wore that heritage like a patriotic badge of honor. He was well educated and a member of the Mercer County Component Medical Society, Medical Society of New Jersey, and the American Medical Society. A Fellow of the American Psychiatric Association and a member of the Neuro-Psychiatric Association. He was even a Diplomat of the American Board of Psychiatry and Neurology.

The English family were sons and daughters of the American Revolution, and for generations they were one of the most prominent and respected families in town. My grandfather served as the chief civil engineer for the City of Trenton and the right-hand man to the mayor. My father had an identical twin brother who was both a well-known and esteemed Princeton attorney and also served as an assistant attorney general for the state of New Jersey.

The house we grew up in was not an ordinary house by any means, and it was once voted the most magnificent home in the city by the local newspaper. It was perched high on a hill overlooking the marvelous Cadwalader Park. Work on the park started in 1887 and it was designed by landscape architect Frederick Law Olmsted, who also designed Central Park in New York City. The English Manor was built in 1928, and all of the bigwigs from the city of Trenton lived in the neighborhoods immediately surrounding it. This was the place to live for anybody who was anybody, or who aspired to be anybody. In fact, two future governors and two state senators lived across the street from the English Manor in their own huge, stately mansions on a hill in

Cadwalader Heights.

Our ivy-covered, castle-like manor had exterior walls of stone imported from England, a slate roof, copper gutters, and sculpted rainspouts. It had cross gables, two massive brick chimneys, leaded glass bay windows, and a stone turret from which you might expect to see an army of archers rain down their arrows or pour hot oil on a storming enemy. Normally a child should feel safe in such a solid environment. Not me. I never could find a safe enough place to hide in the mansion.

Inside the house was a grand entry foyer with a ten-foot vaulted and hand-carved ceiling. The ceiling had gold-etched, hand-painted flowers and, of course, ivy all around its edges. A large and beautiful wooden spiral staircase stood proudly in the middle of the mammoth foyer, winding its way like a corkscrew up the center of the turret. Tall, thin windows circled the staircase, with a landing midway up the stairs serving as a platform for the master of the house to stand and rule over his kingdom.

Off of the foyer in the living room stood a colossal floor-to-ceiling sandstone fireplace with both angelic and demonic figures and *fleur-de-lis* carved over its face. The fireplace hearth alone was four feet tall, four feet wide and four feet deep.

In the living room, on the wall across from the hearth, hung a life-sized oil portrait of the Lord of the Manor, my father, Dr. Harrison Force English. What a great middle name he was given at birth: Force. How fitting and prophetic. In my eyes, Blunt Force would have been even more appropriate.

Harrison was about five feet eight inches tall and of dark complexion. His jet black hair was combed straight back, with a widow's peak in front and a bit of distinguished grey at the sideburns. Harrison was a very good-looking, well-dressed and refined man. He even once modeled hats for a men's magazine.

In the painted image, he wore a look in his eyes that could freeze hell and seemed to follow you around the room. Oil portraits of well-to-do families were common in those days, but Harrison didn't want the family, he only wanted himself in the painting. He was the man of the house and wanted everyone who entered to know that. The portrait made that statement clearly.

In the solarium next to the formal living room, the floor was made entirely of slate. A six-foot fountain in the center of the room poured water from a lion's sculptured mouth into a marble basin. Off the rear entrance of the solarium was a screened porch leading to the grounds of the estate, which overlooked the wondrous one hundred acres of Cadwalader Park. It was on this beautiful screened-in porch that my father and mother hosted many formal white-glove cocktail parties for governors, senators, and various political big shots. Even the town's mayor and his fiancée had an engagement party in the mansion.

The mansion had twenty-six rooms, six bathrooms and six bedrooms. All of the rooms were at least twenty feet long by twenty feet wide, topped by ten-foot ceilings.

To the left of the main entrance were two massive, curved oak doors leading into what was once the formal dining room of the mansion. It served as the private psychiatric office for my father, and his office was completely off limits to his children.

Another curved oak door led into our dining room, which had a floor of earth-colored marble as well as a marble fireplace in the center of one wall. On both sides of the fireplace stood floor-to-ceiling built-in cabinets with French etched leaded glass doors. The cabinets housed all of the formal dishes and glassware. To the rear of this room stood the kitchen, equally large as the other rooms and equipped with all of the latest in culinary hardware and appliances. The back door of the kitchen led to a huge flower garden that wrapped itself around the front and side of the house.

The kitchen had an antique call box mounted on the wall near the entrance. Inside the box was a glass window with small individual tiles lined up inside. Each tile was labeled with a number corresponding to a different room in the house. In the olden days, if someone pushed a button on the wall next to the light switch in another room in the mansion, the tile would drop down and buzz, alerting the servants that their assistance was needed in that room.

Legend has it that the original owner of the house had the materials for its exterior shipped from an ancient castle in England stone by stone as a present for his daughter's wedding. When the daughter broke off her engagement just days before the wedding, the father was so distraught that he hanged himself in the attic of the manor, and he still haunts the place today.

Well, that was the rumor my father told us to keep us fearful and in line whenever he felt malicious, which seemed to me to be often. Sometimes after dinner, for his and my mother's entertainment, my father would order one of us children to walk up to the vast, dark attic and retrieve an object that he had hidden there earlier. None of us wanted to go up there in daylight, let alone on a dark, starless night.

My father would sneak up to the attic ahead of us, moaning and laughing an evil laugh while we were shaking in our shoes trying to find the latest object of his desire in the dark. He locked me up there a few times for what seemed like hours until I cried and begged to be freed from the black prison and he tired of his game. To this day I am claustrophobic and begin to shake and hyperventilate when I am in a closed and dark environment, and I am mentally transported back to the attic of the English Manor.

The other prominent feature of the mansion, which was initially my biggest fright, was the basement, more aptly named the dungeon. I was seven years old when we moved into the house, and to a little boy the cellar seemed like a crypt. It was dark and cold with a permanent musty odor. The basement consisted of five huge, grey rooms with no furniture, empty except for one room in the back, which was filled with the enormous oil furnace that tried its best to heat the house in the wintertime. No matter how hard it pumped and burned the oil, it just couldn't raise the temperature enough to make the house even remotely warm. The walls and floors of the cellar were constructed of concrete with ten-foot ceilings so thick you couldn't hear a sound from upstairs or even from one room to another. All you could hear was an eerie silence and the sound of your own heart beating with fear.

One old, thin, wooden staircase leading down from the kitchen was the only way in or out of the catacomb. The wood was so creaky and the railing so shaky that it seemed ready to collapse at any moment. This was not a fit space for the living unless you were an insect, like a spider—then it was utopia. They seemed to relish the dark and rank environment down there, and what seemed like hundreds of the arachnids thrived up high on the windowsills spinning web after web to catch their prey of unfortunate flies and other unidentifiable insects.

The windows, which were eight feet high on the walls, were small rectangles with frames made of cast iron. They only opened slightly and were out of reach for a young boy hoping to get a breath of fresh air. Being in the basement gave you a strange feeling of being incarcerated in prison.

For a while, we had two dogs that my father kept in the cellar. Marmaduke and Pompadour were large dogs, and I never understood why we had them. No one took them for regular walks or brushed them or gave them baths, and they were never allowed upstairs in the house. They lived in the largest room down in the vault. I suppose every aristocrat needs two large dogs to complete the picture of a stately manor. I think my father missed an opportunity to make a bold statement by posing a dog sitting at attention on either side of him for his oil portrait upstairs. It would have been larger-than-life.

Each week my Saturday afternoon chore was to clean up after the dogs. I hated scraping a week's worth of dog crap off of the concrete floors. Those two dogs each weighed more than one hundred pounds, and all they ever did was eat and go to the bathroom. The stench was horrid because there was no ventilation and I was too small to reach those damned windows. Some of the feces were a week old and some were freshly dropped, making for a revolting texture and odor.

After scraping up the mess with a shovel and placing it in a brown grocery bag for disposal, I had to mop up anything left on the floor. This job was not fit for a ten-year-old boy on a Saturday afternoon. I always thought that I should be outside playing with friends like the rest of the children in the neighborhood.

My father was a meticulous man, and he had very high quality standards for me on this particular chore. He would tell me that I couldn't come upstairs until the floor was spotless. It had to be clean enough to eat off of it. Once after he inspected the job and thought the floor wasn't clean enough to meet his standards, he went dead silent. After what seemed like hours but was just a minute or two he ordered me to stay right where I was, and I thought for sure I was going to be locked down there or get a beating. He quietly went upstairs to eat his dinner, leaving me wondering and worrying the whole time about what my fate would be.

After he finished his meal, he came back down carrying my dinner plate and placed it on the floor in the middle of the stain. I was then ordered to kneel down with my hands held behind my back and eat the food off of the plate with my mouth, like a dog. He stood there and watched me on my knees gagging on each bite until the food was gone, and then he made me lick the plate as clean as the floor should have been in the first place.

CHAPTER TWO

NO LOVE CHILD

The '60s have been dubbed the "cultural decade" of the twentieth century, but not for me. I missed the whole period. Those must have been incredible and exciting times for most people my age. There was the counterculture and social revolution going on all around the English Manor, but time stood still inside.

The '60s were a wonderful era of irresponsibility, excess and flamboyance. The loosening of racism and sexism and the embrace of free love combined with life changing events like Vietnam, Martin Luther King Jr. "I Have a Dream", Stonewall Inn demonstrations in New York City and the Beatles coming through town, I missed it all. I didn't even know that John F. Kennedy was president of the United States until he was assassinated.

Man had first set foot on the moon, Woodstock, Hippies and Flower Power. It all happened while I was just trying to stay out of the way of everyone and keep my sanity.

Of all the children in the house, I was the most out of favor with my father, and I always wondered why. I was a shy and introverted young boy, and because of it I thought that there must have been something mentally wrong with me. I kept to myself and never bothered with anyone and felt inferior to all. I was not permitted to have friends, and I believed that I was just too dumb to recognize what it was about me that was so different from everyone else.

It was as if I didn't exist in this large so-called family, until punishment time—then they certainly knew I existed. Try as I might I just couldn't comprehend what was so bad about me that I was treated so dissimilarly from the other children. My father's favorite nickname for me was Idiot. At that time, I had no way of knowing the ugly truth or the literal and legal meaning behind that simple moniker.

During my entire childhood, I was not allowed to go out after school to visit friends or to have a friend from school come over, so consequently I had no friends. I was never allowed to play any team sports. When I asked my father one year if I could join the local Little League, he admonished me that I was not allowed to play baseball. I had never showed any interest in it before, he said, so why bother now? He informed me that I'd probably be lousy at it, so I should save myself some embarrassment because if I tried I would probably just make an idiot of myself.

I don't recall ever seeing a bit of love in the house between my parents. Growing up I had no example of what real family love meant. I had never seen any hugging, kissing or laughing, or any real healthy interactions. I think consequently that may be why my siblings and I fought with each other much more than typical children.

As I was growing up, an unspoken undercurrent of hostility pervaded the house. We really never lived together as a family. It seemed that we existed with each other physically but not emotionally. In our entire lives, we never connected in a meaningful or loving way, still to this day.

As a youngster, I craved approval that never came. There were no encouraging talks and no support for school activities, so I never participated. I merely came home after school and went to my room until I was called downstairs for dinner, and that was that. Unless, of course, I did something wrong, and then I got more attention than I could ever want or handle. It seemed as though I always had a little mischievousness in me, which routinely got me punished, but for some reason to my chagrin I couldn't help being a little devilish.

One year when I was twelve years old, I tried out for the school choir and was totally surprised to be accepted and chosen for something for the first time ever in my short life. The choir practiced during school lunchtime, so no one at home knew I had made the chorale. Amazingly, I was picked to sing a solo performance during the upcoming school Christmas pageant. I went home and proudly told my father that I had been chosen and was going to sing a Christmas song alone on stage. Instead of being proud of me, he beat me for hiding the fact that I had joined without his permission, and he ordered me to quit the choir. In my first real defiance of him, I sneaked out of the house and ran to school the night of the concert, put on my choir gown and sang my heart out to the audience, all alone. Somehow several days later my father found out that I did it and threatened to admit me to St. Michael's Orphanage, while he was whipping me for disobeying him.

Our upbringing was strict and formal. Dinner was at six o'clock sharp, and we had to dress for the occasion. Any time that we went out in public with our mother or father, we had to dress up. Our hair slicked back, wearing jackets and ties, we were good little bluebloods to be shown off like trophies.

We've all heard of the black sheep of a family, well to me I was the black and blue sheep of the English clan. Over the years, I suffered many whippings and my parents always convinced me that it was my own fault, and I always believed that it was and that I deserved it. I must have broken a dozen pair of my glasses over the years by getting smacked across the face for some simple reason, or for no real reason at all.

I'll never obliterate the memory of the time I was about fourteen years old and was washing the family dinner dishes. I was carrying a stack of eight dinner plates from the kitchen to the dining room to put them in the hutch where they belonged. As I got halfway to the shelves, one of my brothers in a playful way came up behind me and started to tickle me. I begged him to stop until I lost control and dropped all eight plates on the floor. I can still both hear and feel that horrible crash. Each plate broke into hundreds of pieces, and the whole house heard the horrific noise, which was magnified by the marble floor.

My mother and father came running into the room to see me standing alone, surveying the damage at my feet and already crying because I knew I was in serious trouble.

My brother had run to his room via the back stairs, and no one saw him. When I told my mother and father what had happened, my father screamed up the stairs to my brother demanding to know why he would do such a thing to me. He told them he didn't know what I was talking about and that I was a liar. My mother slapped me hard across the face for daring to make up a lie about my brother, breaking my glasses once again, and then I got the belt from my father for being stupid enough to carry that many dishes at one time. It was after all, my fault and I was an idiot for doing it.

Back then, if the public had learned some of our family's secrets, a scandal would have resulted. Reputation was everything, especially for a family with our tony lineage. If any of our many secrets became public, God knew what catastrophe would happen and who would be hurt or could possibly be destroyed by the revelations.

I always seemed a little different from the other siblings and never understood why. For instance, I was the only one in the family who was naturally left-handed, but my father wasn't having any of that. He believed that being left-handed was the work of the devil and that it caused psychiatric and developmental disorders and schizophrenia. As a cure for my evil left-handedness he made me write two hundred words each night with my right hand. This went on for years. Today I am ambidextrous and I can do almost everything with either hand. I think that had I been allowed to play baseball, I might have been a good switch hitter. Still, I continue to favor my left hand for writing. It proves that you can't fight Mother Nature after all; and despite the hours and hours of forced writing I remain a left-handed writer today.

All of that compulsory writing took up a lot of my time, and it affected my schoolwork in a negative way. It made me a poor student, which definitely contributed to my low self-esteem. It also made me a resentful child, but I kept it to myself because the consequences of any negativity or of my feeling sorry for myself would have been horrific.

My younger brother was the chosen one of the family and a mama's boy to boot. He looked just like Mom. He was a good, quiet kid with a ton of artistic talent, but he was very emotional. I often wondered if he ever knew the family story, dirty secrets and all, and if that is what damaged him emotionally.

Everything came naturally to him and he eventually created many wonderful artistic sculptures that were displayed publicly. He was definitely the talent of the family.

As a young adult, he sculpted a life-sized bronze angel that still stands on the corner of Perry and Warren Streets on the spot where George Washington fought the British. Everyone loved the angel, and the only problem the city had with it was that he made the angel not only life-sized but anatomically correct. It wasn't long before the city asked him to sculpt a fig leaf to place over the private parts of the angel due to the public uproar the statue caused and the fact that it stood right in front of an elementary school. My brother fought the demand to cover up the offending parts for artistic reasons until the city threatened to pull the angel down and he finally relented. He begrudgingly added a fig leaf to shield the public's prying and offended eyes and then he promptly moved out of the city, never to return.

Only a couple of people know that the model for that nude angel was a longtime New Jersey state senator's son and that the boy's life-sized personal parts were now pointing forever towards the State Capitol building, where his dad was inside presiding over New Jersey's lawmaking.

My brother wound up creating special effects in Hollywood for the movies *Gremlins* and *Beetlejuice* and worked for Disney rebuilding Gothic structures after they suffered a disastrous fire. He once told me of a movie scene he worked on some thirty years before special effects were as technically advanced as they are now. The scene is in an operating room, and a surgeon is making his first cut into a patient. Suddenly the doctor accidentally slices into an artery and blood squirts everywhere, soaking the nurses and everyone in the operating room. My brother was perched under the table snickering with a tube that he had rigged to squirt bags of fake blood on cue, and of course, he over did it.

Unfortunately, my brother turned into a loner, drifting from state to state, and he died far too young as a recluse. I wish that he had lived long enough for me to share this book with him, as he would have loved it and probably added some craziness to it himself.

The youngest child of our family was the only daughter. She was a beautiful blonde girl who had my mother's looks, abilities and talent. She could charm anyone just by smiling at them. I got beaten badly by my father once because I couldn't spell her name correctly. I misspelled it on a homemade birthday card that I made for her one year, and I got a belt whipping for it. I had to write her name two hundred times—with my right hand, of course.

My sister who is six years younger than me was one tough tomboy and even rode a Yamaha motorcycle when she got older. She had to be tough as the youngest of six and the only daughter. She was the princess of the family, and I loved my sister dearly.

Growing up in this environment was definitely a bad time for me, but there were a few good times as well, and those good times were my salvation.

Almost every other Sunday in the spring and summer months we all piled into my father's big Chrysler Town Car and drove for about an hour to our Uncle Art's farm in Hopewell.

Hopewell was an old town discovered by the Lenape Indians, who lived on the banks of a stony brook in the 1600s until the Europeans arrived and forced them to move west. In 1776, Hopewell was occupied by the British when General George Washington crossed the Delaware River and defeated them in the battles of Trenton and Princeton. John Hart, one of the signers of the Declaration of Independence, was born in Hopewell, and General Washington actually crossed the Delaware from Pennsylvania into Hopewell on that eventful Christmas Eve, not into Trenton as most believe.

The other claim to fame for little historic Hopewell was the 1932 kidnapping and murder of the 20-month-old son of Charles and Anne Lindbergh; the child's body was never found causing many people over the years to claim they were the Lindbergh baby and heir to the fortune. Still today there is great debate about the kidnapping and the "Trial of the Century" of Bruno Hauptmann that will haunt the quaint town of Hopewell forever.

I lived for our family's occasional but wonderful Sunday trips to Hopewell. When I say that we piled into the Chrysler, I mean that we fit two adults and six children in that car. Five of us boys would squeeze into the mammoth back seat that somehow didn't feel so huge, and my mother had my sister sit in the front seat between her and my father.

My Uncle Art was a magnificent and gregarious man and always treated each of us children well. For some unknown reason he had a soft spot for me, and thankfully he seemed to want to spend time alone with me whenever he could. I later realized that he knew the truth about how I was being treated at home and was doing his best to make my life more enjoyable. He succeeded.

He was a large man and a larger role model for me. He was a skilled tradesman, and his day job was as a machinist at the De Laval Steam Turbine Company in Trenton. De Laval opened in Trenton in 1900 and produced the world's largest turbine engines, pumps and compressors. They employed more than two thousand people, and my Uncle Art was key to keeping the factory running, making parts for the turbines to keep them churning smoothly.

He was extremely talented and creative, and he loved his sizeable historic farm, which sat on the top of Stony Brook Mountain in Hopewell. The farmhouse was a white clapboard structure with a small front porch and an old-fashioned wrought iron triangle dinner bell hanging in the corner, a wrought iron rod attached by a leather strap hung from it waiting to be pressed into action. Out front stood a massive hundred-year-old oak tree with a rope tied to its thickest limb and a rusted red metal swing swaying in the wind.

The farm had a substantial vegetable garden planted on the side of the house, making the homestead self-sustainable. Next to the garden sat an ancient well with an antique pump that was once used to fill a wooden bucket to supply water for the farmhouse. In later years when the old house was equipped with indoor plumbing and running water, the pump was used to irrigate the garden vegetables.

Each Sunday that we visited, I would leap out of the car and sprint to the pump to fill the bucket with water for the vegetables. It was my job and a chore I loved to do because I knew it was the start of my great adventure on the farm, even if I would be there only for a few hours, a few days a year.

Uncle Art adored children, but he had none of his own. He would have been an outstanding father. Any child would have been lucky to have him for a dad, and he loved to play with and cherish children.

In the summer months, Uncle Art would erect an oversized above-ground swimming pool near the farmhouse. He would sit under the shade of an old oak tree watching us swim and play for hours with a big smile on his face as he served as our lifeguard.

He had a large two-story barn on the property that housed his grey 1950s-era Plymouth sedan with its big, wide whitewall tires. Inside the barn sat a large green John Deere tractor and a black Ford pickup that he drove to work every day.

As a young teenager, I was fascinated by anything with wheels, and that tractor had some seriously massive wheels. When we first started visiting Uncle Art, the rear tractor wheels were bigger than I was. It was really a simple machine, but to me that tractor was a marvel of engineering. It was painted a dull green—almost a military green—with a generous sprinkling of rust and holes. Nothing on the machine was shiny anymore. It was routinely used for everything from plowing the fields and gardens to plowing the snow on the long driveway leading into the farm.

The tractor was long and rectangular with two pipes that looked like chimneys coming out of the top. The engine compartment had no hood so you could see the moving parts running. Above the huge rear wheels were two headlights, one on each side, each as big as my head. At night they lit up a field like it was daytime.

Between the wheels was a small metal seat shaped like a pear with holes drilled into it to keep a driver's backside cooler in the hot summer. It was mounted onto a single large rod that acted as a spring to ease some of the bumps for the driver. Uncle Art would hook a small wagon to the tractor, fill it with hay and give us hayrides around the farm while wearing a big straw hat to shield his balding head from the sun. He was quite a sight bouncing up and down on the spring seat, laughing and watching us enjoy the ride.

The barn had a second floor loft that had been a hayloft in the old days and now served as my uncle's workshop. He was an amateur woodcarver, and his carvings always looked realistic, almost lifelike. Every time we drove to the farm there was some new, amazing sight to see. Pulling into the long gravel road leading to the farm, we saw a field full of dozens of cows. What was unique about Uncle Art's farm was that the cows were made out of wood and painted to look realistic. He had mounted each of them on a metal stake driven into the ground, with a hinge behind each cow's tail. As the wind blew, the cows shifted back and forth and the old rusty cowbells hanging around their necks clanged a friendly greeting to all who came to visit the farmstead.

Across the driveway was another garden, only this garden, unlike the one I watered, was handmade by Uncle Art. There were dozens of wooden flowers, each flower painted a different color. The petals would spin in the wind like a pinwheel.

Scattered in various spots under the trees or in the fields were life-sized farmers also made of wood. They were tending the cows, weeding the gardens, or just hanging out and waving to people who passed the fields. Each was unique. One farmer would tip his hat each time the wind blew, and another would bend up and down as if weeding the garden. Another sawed wood, and yet another tended a hoe. When the wind blew, it was like taking a ride on "It's a Small World" at Disneyland.

Half of the farm was covered with acres and acres of dense forest. My uncle let me borrow a bow and arrow from the barn, and I was transported back in time and hiding out in Sherwood Forest. He only gave me one arrow because I had lost a few my first time out. We pledged to keep that to ourselves so my father wouldn't beat me for it.

I would wander for hours and hours alone in those woods

fantasizing that I was Robin Hood searching for the Sheriff of Nottingham. I would explore and stay alone in those woods all day until someone rang the old dinner bell to alert everyone that supper was ready. You could hear that robust and distinct ring for miles.

My Uncle Art knew how much I loved the woods, and every once in a while I came across a new surprise. He had wooden deer, handmade squirrels and owls with bull's-eyes painted on them all strategically placed for me to shoot. I became a good shot, because if I lost that arrow I'd be done and I wouldn't be able to play anymore. I could shoot that arrow anywhere I wanted to on a target, although I admit that I only took the easy, close shots to avoid having to search for the arrow in the leaves.

It was my job to search the woods for signs of hunters who were not allowed on the farm, and I'd tell Uncle Art where their deer blinds were hidden so he could destroy them and post "No Hunting" signs. I could spot those hidden deer blinds from hundreds of feet away.

Uncle Art loved barbecuing hamburgers on his charcoal grill for all of us. It wasn't really a grill, but a metal barrel cut in half with a heavy mesh wire screen placed on top. He would work the grill for hours while his wife, Aunt Rachel, would make a fresh vegetable salad straight from the garden along with corn on the cob that we would pick and shuck. Then, for dessert, we would have fresh apple pie made from apples that we'd picked off of their apple trees. Farm living was something I always admired.

Spending time on the farm and in the woods was the only good part of my childhood. I was fortunate to have Uncle Art looking out for me. I only saw him when we visited Hopewell about a dozen times each year, but each and every time was memorable, and he and that enchanted place live in my heart forever. Every child should have an Uncle Art.

CHAPTER THREE

MOTHER

My mother, Elizabeth Stapf English, was a stay-at-home mom most of her adult life. She was absolutely beautiful in a Sophia Loren sort of way, and everywhere she went men would turn their heads and ogle her or whistle at her.

She loved the attention men bestowed on her, and she would smile and wave and sometimes stop and flirt with any man who had the nerve to say something to her. She took her flirting further sometimes and allowed men to hold her hand or put an arm around her, and sometimes she rewarded their forwardness with a kiss on the cheek.

The kids in school jokingly voted her the sexiest mom in school because she was not only beautiful, but she also wore tight clothes, even when she was at the school. My mother seemed to feel the need to dazzle men and flabbergast women. She thrived on the jealousy of others.

She had strawberry blonde hair and kept her body in great shape until later in life. She was smart and talented. She could create anything, and she could do everything that she put her mind to as well as anyone could. Over the years and with no formal training, she taught herself to oil paint and created several beautiful and professional-looking portraits. She learned to paint first by painting flowers and bowls of fruit, and then she moved on to the more difficult task of painting people. As her skills began to progress, her repertoire including painting nudes. She especially liked painting live nude models.

She once hand-built a retaining wall four-foot-high and forty-foot-long out of hand cut flagstone for her garden at the mansion. She tended to vast, exotic gardens. She was an expert seamstress and hand-stitched everything we needed, from curtains to the clothes on our backs. It seemed that she could teach herself to do anything.

Mom spoke with a heavy German accent that stayed with her all of her life. In fact, she worked hard at keeping her German enunciation as pronounced as possible. She purposely used her accent to her advantage in both her flirting and her mocking. She knew it made her more attractive, and it allowed her to get away with saying almost anything inappropriate. She used to call my father's brother a "prostitutor," knowing very well that he was actually a respected attorney and a "prosecutor."

I never knew much about Mom. I didn't know where she came from, where her family was or even what her maiden name was until much later in life. The past wasn't discussed at our house, and somehow I knew not to ask about it. I wasn't allowed to know anything about her family for fear that I might ask too many questions about what went on in her past. If I had known, I might have slipped up and told someone outside the family what I had learned. We were told a thousand times, "Children should be seen and not heard." The message was clear: Keep your mouth shut and mind your own business, and don't tell anyone outside the family anything about our personal business.

I did know one thing about my mother. She had a huge mean streak, and I never wanted to get on her bad side.

In my early memories, back in the 1950s we had a live-in domestic servant named Maria. Maria somehow, through my mother's family, came from Germany to work as a nanny, but she was really more of an indentured servant. She was probably in her twenties and was very nice to the children. She kept to herself and did her job of waking us up in the mornings for school, making breakfast, seeing us to the bus stop, and then cleaning the house. When she finished cleaning she would go to her room in the attic, never leaving the confines of the house. I never knew whether Maria was related to us by blood. Maria didn't speak a word of English, but she quickly learned how to say "Please don't hit me again" in English.

Maria got punished if the dishes were dirty or if there was dust in the house. Any infraction or mistake, or anything out of place in the house, and she got cracked. Once she needed stitches across her forehead after my mother hit her on the head with a cast iron ice cream scoop. The scoop cut a deep gash in her forehead, and her face was covered in blood; it was the first time I had ever seen so much blood. I don't remember what little infraction she committed to deserve it, but immediately after that episode Maria was packed up and sent back to Germany, even before the stitches were out.

I can never forget sneaking up the stairs and peeking in the doorway of Maria's bedroom in the attic. Maria's back was to me, and she was packing her beat-up leather suitcase, her head bandaged up like a mummy, crying and shaking uncontrollably.

I think I was the only one of the six children Maria said goodbye to before my father and mother put her in their car and drove her away. Probably because we were kindred souls of a sort, with all of the beatings both of us experienced.

While she was being loaded into the car, I peeked out of the living room window, and Maria gave me one last sorrowful look and a wave goodbye before being chauffeured away forever. Maybe that strange, depressed look on her face was because she was going back to Germany, or maybe she knew that now it was I alone who would get all of the beatings in the house.

Many years later, what I found out about my mother shocked me. She was a native German who grew up in a town called Pforzheim, near Stuttgart, during World War II. Pforzheim was targeted by Allied bombers heavily and the whole town eventually was flattened, killing thousands of people. She was drafted into duty during the war at sixteen years old for civil defense work. The job they assigned her was to chart the location of Allied planes on a giant glass map so the German army could track them and plan their defense accordingly. She later worked as an interpreter for high-ranking American officers during the American occupation, as she spoke English fluently.

She told me a story many years later. One day, she switched lunch breaks with a friend at her civil defense job, and there was an air raid. She said the sky was quickly peppered with Allied bombers. Sirens started wailing, and all of the townspeople were running in every direction trying to find cover or get to the nearest bomb shelter. She wound up in the basement of a bakery crammed in with the baker, his family and a few customers.

After the bombs stopped dropping and things had quieted down, they went upstairs to a ruined shell of a bakery. It had been hit by one of the bombs and had been destroyed. One wall was gone, and burned pastries and pies dripped off the other partial walls. She walked back toward where she had worked, and she said she couldn't believe her eyes as she surveyed the carnage. It looked as though the entire town had been destroyed.

Climbing over debris, she finally reached the civil defense building only to find that it was no longer there. It had been bombed by the same Allied planes she'd been tracking. She said she lost everything she owned and everyone she knew in that air raid and that if she hadn't switched shifts with her girlfriend it would have been her lying in the debris with the rest of the corpses.

She vowed to herself then and there, among the rubble and ruins, to leave Germany and make her way to the United States of America, the land of promise and opportunity. She knew she would get there by any means necessary, and she certainly did.

CHAPTER FOUR

TRENTON MADHOUSE

My father, Dr. Harrison Force English, was the senior psychiatrist at the Trenton Psychiatric Hospital and a diplomat of the American Board of Psychiatry. In that lofty position, he was charged with the care, safety and security of the hospital's patients. He was supposed to supervise and maintain psychiatric order at the institute, but in reality he presided over mental mayhem at both the asylum and at his home, the English Manor.

Originally named the New Jersey State Lunatic Asylum, the institution was the first of its kind built in the United States. This hospital was a warehouse-style asylum for New Jersey's criminally insane. It also served as a dumping ground for the state's indigent patients left to rot by thoughtless families, vengeful spouses, inept doctors or the staggeringly unjust judicial system of the times.

The Trenton Psychiatric Hospital was home to many a poor soul too crazy or too sick to understand their surroundings or—even worse—sane enough to know they were trapped in a living hell with no chance of escape.

The asylum was built in 1848 on seven hundred acres of serene meadows and was constructed from reddish sandstone obtained from local quarries, giving it an eerie appearance. The dark Gothic construction of the insane asylum was surrounded and hidden by hundreds of massive protective oak trees. The trees were deliberately placed there to keep the patients in and the prying eyes of the public out. The structure was home not only to some of the most criminally insane patients ever known, but also to some of the country's most mentally disturbed doctors and staff.

The proud Trenton institution attracted many admirers and supporters. At the time, little did these folks know about the true horrors that hid behind the luxurious grandeur? The venerated establishment was aptly referred to locally as The Trenton Madhouse, first because it housed some of the most insane patients and criminals and second due to the equally deranged physicians, administrators and so-called mental health treatment professionals at the asylum.

For some patients, rotting away in their cells may have been preferable to the inhuman experimentation and physical brutality that the ivy-covered and penitentiary-like walls concealed from the outside world until many years later.

One of the first accounts of the evils of the Trenton Madhouse came to light in 1905, when typhoid fever was rampant in the institution and threatened to spill out and overcome the city of Trenton. At that time, the hospital was run by Dr. John Ward.

With a *laissez-faire* attitude, Ward let the madhouse run itself in a true "the inmates are running the asylum" scenario. His claim to notoriety was that he allowed patients to be shackled or restrained for years on end without a care about their terror, discomfort, fate, or rights.

The occasional visitor to the asylum would first sense the abject despair that was prevalent throughout the institution. The visitor would then see neglected patients sitting in their own feces in the hallways, rocking themselves in a futile effort to find some measure of comfort. Some patients would bang their heads against the walls incessantly.

There were rumors that the elderly patients were being raped and brutalized by attendants who may have been more insane than they were. Some reports said nude patients were hosed down with freezing water while staff members stood by laughing.

And then came the final and ultimate mistreatment of the patients, their burial. The traumatized bodies of patients who had died during their so-called healthcare treatments were unceremoniously dumped in unmarked mass graves in the woods on the asylum grounds just behind the majestic building. Reports that were once kept hidden eventually shed light on routine beatings, botched abortions, starvation, and desperate suicides, which may have been the only way one could escape the facility.

Dr. Ward at first ignored the rampant sickness and death occurring under his reign. He overlooked reports of illness even when his own staff began to succumb. Ward disregarded safety reports from audits of the facility and had the audacity to claim that even though inspections found human and animal waste within the kitchens of the hospital, it didn't threaten food handling or the milk supply, which he himself partook of daily.

It turned out that both the patients and the staff of the Trenton Psychiatric Hospital were drinking water tainted with their own feces. Water treatment was not a high priority for the hospital or for Administrator Ward. After all, did anyone really care about the souls within? Wasn't "out of sight, out of mind" a good philosophy? Hundreds of patients perished, but it drew little attention. They were an embarrassment to society, after all.

It was only when some of the staff members took ill themselves and their own personal physicians outside of the hospital diagnosed an outbreak of typhoid did the town fathers begin to take notice of the serious health issues. When they finally realized their own families could be at risk of an epidemic, the city administrators took action and fired Ward.

After the abrupt removal of John Ward, came a new reign of terror for the patients by the name of Dr. Henry Cotton. History refers to him as "The Most Frightening Psychiatrist," and he became one of the most infamous and terrifying doctors our country had ever seen. As their bad luck would have it, the poor souls of the Trenton Madhouse were now out of the proverbial frying pan and into the fire.

Dr. Cotton had a curious theory that insanity was caused by an infection somewhere within the body. He strongly believed that he could cure insanity by removing any body parts that contained bacteria and disease, a kind of one-stop shopping for madness relief.

Historically documented accounts of the asylum under his regime speak of terrified patients being dragged, hysterically screaming, into the mad doctor's private operating room, urinating on themselves in the hallways out of fear, and being beaten into submission until they were unconscious and could no longer fight the horrific fate of the doctor's scalpel.

As head of the asylum, Henry Cotton was God and could do anything he wanted without question and without repercussion. After all, back in the 1940s, who was smarter than a psychiatrist, and who had the audacity to question the doctor's tactics? Anyone who tried would be made a fool for challenging such an educated man.

Following his perverse theories, Dr. Cotton proposed that an insane person's teeth were the first place that an infection, and therefore insanity, would set in. The doctor would strap patients to a gurney in his private operating room and extract all of their teeth, one by one.

If, after a healing period of a few weeks, a patient wasn't cured of insanity, the doctor would perform a second operation, this time to remove the patient's tonsils.

If the removal of the patient's tonsils didn't work and they were still insane, he would schedule more operations to remove a patient's sinuses, and then their testicles, ovaries, gall bladders, stomachs, spleens, cervix and, finally, their colons. Dr. Cotton was determined to get to the bottom of the infection and cure these patients of insanity no matter what the cost.

Salivating for the ultimate recognition of a Nobel Peace Prize, and with no one of authority gutsy enough to dispute his findings, Dr. Cotton reported to his bosses at the New Jersey State Legislature that he had an incredible eighty-five percent cure rate for his patients.

In later years, after investigations took place, it was found that more than half the patients under his care had died. Amazingly, Dr. Cotton had the audacity to put these deaths in his "win" column because, to him, those patients no longer suffered from their afflictions. Since they were dead, they obviously had been cured of their insanity, proving the old saying that liars can figure and figures can lie.

So consumed was he with his own theories that insanity was

simply caused by infection and that the first place infection set in was the teeth, the doctor removed all the teeth of his own children so they would never go insane.

One day the doctor's thirteen-year-old son had the misfortune of disagreeing with his dad, as teens are apt to do, and the boy was punished with the removal of his colon, an effort to cure his insane tendencies of disagreeing with dear old Dad. After all, the child must have been crazy to disagree with his father, a psychiatrist.

Records show that Dr. Cotton and his staff presided over more than two thousand major operations, almost all of which were illegal and unnecessary. As a psychiatrist, he had no surgical training and was not a licensed surgeon. He credited his surgical ability to having watched schooled surgeons perform procedures in medical school many years before, and he actually bragged about his carving skills.

What ultimately brought an end to Dr. Cotton's mistreatment of the patients were his shameless ambition and a sort of P.T. Barnum-esque style of promoting both himself and his work. The desire for fame and prestige lured him to a level of shameless self-aggrandizement previously unknown in the medical profession. The spotlight brought the notice of the public, the government and his peers. One such peer, a Dr. N. Katzenelbogen, once visited the hospital and wrote:

"I felt sad, seeing hundreds of people without teeth. Only a very few have teeth. The hospital takes care as to the pulling out of teeth, but does not provide false teeth. ... The extraction of teeth does great harm to those who cannot afford to pay for a set of false teeth, and these patients are numerous. While in the hospital they suffer from indigestion ... not being able to masticate their food."

The patients being unable to digest their food without their teeth was music to Dr. Cotton's ears, as it offered him the opportunity to continue to play surgeon and demonstrate more of his surgical prowess.

After more than twenty years, Dr. Cotton was finally removed from his position as head of the asylum. With a new administrator in place, the asylum ended its horrific practice of needless surgery and instead began experimenting with hallucinogenic drugs and hypnosis for treatment of psychosis. Patients were now heavily medicated to keep them under control, like in the novel and movie *One Flew Over the Cuckoo's Nest*.

While the new treatment with drugs may have been better than the ghastly operations that Dr. Cotton performed, new reports poured in detailing accounts of horrific conditions at the hospital. These documented reports related that the Trenton State Hospital staff was specializing in brutality and that the uncomprehending patients were being neglected, beaten and abandoned in lonely wards where they sometimes weren't fed or even clothed.

Some reports uncovered that patients didn't shower for months or were left lying in their own filth. Other reports said the hospital forcibly medicated patients with massive doses of mind-altering drugs, sometimes administered by painful intramuscular injection, without any meaningful medical oversight and without due process of law for the poor souls interned at the hospital.

Back then, in the 1950s and 1960s, patients didn't have any legal right to refuse medication, so if a psychiatrist ordered it, the person was doped regardless of their desires. Sometimes this meant a lifetime sentence and a never ending trip to La-La Land.

The problem with this new "medication model" came to light in later studies that proved sufferers of dementia, personality disorders, head injuries and other like conditions do not respond well to psychotropic drugs. This new practice turned the Trenton Psychiatric Hospital into a bizarre asylum of zombie-like patients aimlessly wandering the grounds. Patients were befuddled, beaten and drugged into submission. The institution continued to earn its popular moniker The Trenton Madhouse.

Soon after the reign of Dr. Henry Cotton the mental and physical care was meted out under the steadfast eye of one of the Trenton Madhouse's newest soon-to-be-infamous physician, a local-born, blue-blooded doctor named Harrison Force English, my father.

CHAPTER FIVE

IDIOT

My father never seemed to care for me, and his distain was obvious. I never knew until later in life why he disliked like me out of all of the six children, although I was a little devilish in a Dennis-the-Menace sort of way. When I did find out the reason for his feelings, it made perfect sense. He never had a kind word or a word of encouragement for me in our sixteen years together. In fact, my father went out of his way to say mean and degrading things to me. His favorite nickname for me was Idiot. Growing up, I assumed it was a simple, nasty moniker that he'd picked out of the air for me. I supposed that he just liked the word's demeaning and humiliating ring.

While researching this book, I stumbled across an old roster of patients admitted into the Trenton Lunatic Asylum. The roster consisted of two columns: One column listed a patient's name, and the other column had a one-word reason for the person's commitment into the asylum. Most patients were simply stamped "insane" beside their name, but many had the title "idiot" next to theirs. This aroused my curiosity, and I did some research on exactly what the word "idiot" meant according to the State of New Jersey in those times. There it was in black and white. The term "idiot" was the legal definition for "mentally disabled boys."

When I read this declaration, chills went up my spine. If a psychiatrist labeled a young boy an "idiot," that boy could be committed to the Trenton Psychiatric Hospital without anyone questioning the process. In my father's day at the asylum, that boy could be permanently medicated with mind-altering drugs and locked away for the rest of his life.

I'd thought he was just being mean when he used to threaten to have me committed to the institution. He was serious, and it could have been my fate to be one of the lost and mentally disabled boys at the asylum.

In addition to routinely threatening to have me committed to the asylum, my father had another terrifying scenario for me: foster care. The threat was St. Michael's Orphanage, officially known as St. Michael's Orphan Asylum and Industrial School. He often threatened to have me committed there as well, whenever he felt that I was misbehaving.

One Sunday afternoon I saw a group of boys from St. Michael's getting out of a school bus at a Catholic church down the block from our house. The church was called Blessed Sacrament, and both the orphanage and the church had school basketball teams that played each other once in a while.

One day my father noticed me looking at the children as they were being ordered off the bus in single file by the Sisters of the Order. He asked me if I knew who they were, and I said yes. I confessed that a new boy in my class at school used to live at the orphanage and had told me scary stories about how he was treated there. I unwittingly told my father one of my biggest fears in life, and his threats to have me sent to the orphanage started almost immediately and never stopped. One day it was the asylum, the next day the orphanage.

Soon after I told him what I knew of the orphanage, my father presented me with a picture that frightened me to no end. In the black and white photo stood the orphanage, a huge, five-story Gothic building that looked similar to the Trenton Madhouse. The picture depicted dozens of young boys standing at attention to the left of a long driveway leading up to the orphanage and dozens of young girls standing at attention to the right side. They all had the same stoic look on their faces and were standing with their arms straight at their sides, all wearing the same clothes and looking like statues instead of happy children.

Looming over the children were nuns in their black and white religious habits with ropes tied around their waists, looking as strict as they probably were. The only thing I knew, aside from the stories of those nuns beating children into submission, was that this place wasn't somewhere a young boy wanted to be. My father described it as a cold, cruel and dark place where children were fed nothing but bread and soup. It was a place where unwanted children were sent, never to be seen or heard from again. I was sufficiently terrified, and he knew it and loved it.

My father had a daily routine. He would come home from work every day exactly at five o'clock, stand at the kitchen counter and gulp down a full glass of Calvert Extra Blended Whiskey on the rocks while reading his evening newspaper. That drink and that newspaper both had damned well better be there waiting for him when he got home, or a beating would follow. It was one of my chores, so it was my beating.

If the newspaper had been read by anyone first or was even unfolded, or if the whiskey had been poured too soon and got watery from the ice, or was poured too late and wasn't cold enough, bam! He made sure someone was always waiting for him to walk through the door when he came home from the hospital. Unlike other fathers who had a wife or children lovingly awaiting their arrival and eager to see them, he had me cowering and dreading his arrival, and he relished it that way. He needed it that way to feel superior. I had to stand at attention like a soldier whenever he walked into a room until I was dismissed.

His favorite and often repeated line was, "Children should be seen and not heard." We must have heard that line thousands of times over the years. I think he believed that children were servants who were put on earth to tend to the needs of their parents, nothing more or nothing less.

If I expressed an opinion about any subject, he would say with a hardened face, "Children should be seen and not heard." If I tried to inject myself into a conversation between adults or even among my brothers and sister, I was either humiliated or slapped. I was taught that I couldn't have an opinion about anything because it would be the wrong opinion. It was best to keep my mouth shut and not make a fool out of myself.

Wounds heal and physical pain ends, but mental pain can

forever be etched into a person's mind. Dr. English was a professional at doling out mental pain. He knew how and when to use his words as weapons and just what to say and when to say it to hurt an impressionable young child as badly as possible. These verbal bashings were sometimes worse than the beatings, and the pain lasted longer. Some of his oral thumping still hurts, and that pain has lasted a lifetime.

Harrison went through a couple of bottles of whiskey per week, and he was a mean drunk. After a couple of drinks it became his job to think of some reason to thrash me. There is nothing more horrific than a child being beaten both mentally and physically by a drunken psychiatrist who seems to delight in every minute of it.

The ritual played over and over again: "Let me see the two hundred words you wrote today." "Are your chores finished?" "What have you learned today?" All scowled directly at me. I was constantly scared, and I knew I had better have an answer fast. If he didn't like an answer—and I swear he was looking for reasons not to like my answers—I got a beating. I would practice alone in my room, answering the same questions over and over in the mirror every day so I would have the right answer to please him and stop the beatings. But there was never any pleasing him. I would break out in a cold sweat when it was nearing time for him to come home. I always wondered what was wrong with me for hating and fearing the very sight of my father.

How mean or uncaring was my father? Well, he left one heck of a public legacy. Thirty years after his death, the State of New Jersey investigated the treatment of patients at the state's psychiatric hospitals during both Dr. Cotton's and my father's tenure. They found hundreds of old graves out in the back of the asylum near the woods of the property. The graves had four-digit markers with numbers etched into their flat tops corresponding with listings in the hospital log books. It turned out that when some of the patients died, the hospital staff was ordered to simply wrap them in a sheet, dig a hole and bury them on the grounds behind the hospital.

Those fading grave markers were all that was left of the indigent psychiatric patients from long ago. They were encased in pine boxes, wrapped in body bags, and then buried shoulder-to-shoulder in the ground. Some of them were buried only in plastic sheets. In 2009, New Jersey State Senator Richard Codey, who conducted the investigation, said, *"This is all these former patients have to show for their lives—a number. This is a stark reminder of society's attitude toward the mentally ill at one point in our history."*

The senator's last point really drove it home for me. Even though not all of the inmates were criminals he stated in the newspaper The Star Ledger: *"It was like these people committed a crime. They were treated in life and in death like they did something wrong."*

Senator Cody's plan is to undo the wrong by restoring the gravesites and creating an electronic registry of the deceased patients from long ago so that they will no longer be buried in anonymity. Under the senator's plan relatives of the patients could contact the state Department of Human Services and access the electronic registry helping to find where their ancestors are buried so that they could give them the dignity that they deserve.

That hit me hard. That was exactly the way my father had always treated me—like a criminal. I grew up being told that I was always wrong, an idiot, and that all I would ever amount to was a garbage collector. I remember thinking, but never daring to ask, what was so wrong with being a garbage collector? It seemed like an honest living to me.

I wonder how someone of sane mind could dig a hole and bury these people without a ceremony, a prayer or a headstone, and without making any attempt to reach their families or to document how or why they died. How could a doctor who took the Hippocratic Oath, who cared for and got to personally know his patients for sometimes years on end, just callously order their bodies dumped out back in the woods and then go home and sleep?

I can't count the number of times during my youth that my father threatened to have me committed to that psychiatric hospital. He used to warn me that if I didn't straighten out to his liking, all he had to do was sign the papers and off I would go. He promised me that no one would question my being admitted, and that I would never again see the light of day.

I often wonder how close I got and how many times he thought not only of committing me to the asylum, but also of burying me in the woods along with those insane patients and the rest of the "idiots."

CHAPTER SIX

BOARD OF EDUCATION

Dinner in the mansion was always a somber occasion. It was especially an adventure after my father had his evening Scotch. It's no wonder I was so thin all my life; I was afraid to eat. Eight people would quietly sit around a ten-foot rectangular table with very little conversation—no one dared speak. There was nothing but dead silence at the English family dinner table.

My father sat at the head of the table like the lord of his manor, and he ruled his kingdom with an iron fist. A large plank of wood from the corner of the massive dinner table was repeatedly broken off, glued and re-glued. Whenever my father was angry about something, which was often, he would bang his fist on the table hard enough to split the wood. At what seemed like every meal, he would look at me and bark, "Harold, did you do your chores?" "Harold, did you do your homework?" "Harold, did you practice your writing right-handed?" And the worst, "Harold did you eat your vegetables?" I knew he was looking for a reason to let out some aggression from his day at the asylum, and I also knew I would be his target.

Have you eaten your vegetables? Oh, those vegetables! Like most kids, I hated green vegetables. My parents could have tried to cook them another way, or perhaps hid them in some other food to get me to eat them. Instead, my father simply walked over behind my chair, grabbed my head, forced open my mouth with his fingers and shoved the vegetables in.

How he must have savored the feeling of absolute power when he did that. Whenever it happened, my mother, brothers and sister would start eating their vegetables pronto. He shoved those veggies deep down my throat until my mouth was stuffed completely full and he couldn't cram any more in. I would try to swallow, or I gagged and coughed them up. Then he would drag me into the kitchen and beat me for ruining everyone's dinner. Next he would make me clean up the mess that I had made, screaming that I was a filthy, disgusting idiot who belonged in the asylum.

Today I can't stand the smell of certain vegetables being cooked, and I gag when I do. Brussels sprouts were the worst. As an adult I discovered that I love eating vegetables raw, and now I eat them all the time, but if they are cooked I still gag and can't swallow them. Some things I just never got over.

Sometimes my father used an old military riding crop to dole out his discipline. That was the worst of the many objects I was beaten with while growing up in the English household. It was made of some sort of wood with a small steel tip on the end. As my father whacked me, it would bend like a golf club and then whip.

The more times he hit me, the more bend in the whip, and the more pain. He was an expert with this thrasher and knew exactly what he was doing because he only hit me relatively lightly three or four times in any one session. Any harder or any more than that and he would have torn both my clothes and my flesh, drawing blood. Once, when the crop wasn't convenient enough, he used a long-handled wooden shower brush, which broke after only a couple of swings against my back. Then I had to work off the cost of the brush doing extra chores around the house because, of course, it was the idiot's fault that the handle broke.

Harrison relished it when I cried. He felt empowered. Unfortunately for me, I was such a stubborn child that I didn't want to give him the satisfaction of my crying, and I always held out as long as I could. That defiance caused me to be beaten much longer than if I had cried right away. Clearly the beatings were my fault, as I could have stopped them by crying on the first strike.

I'll never forget one of the many days when I thought about ending my life and came close to doing so. One Saturday afternoon after a particularly painful Friday night beating and when no one else was home, I went searching for the riding crop. I was going to try to break it or hide it so I wouldn't have to suffer its wrath anymore. I knew my father kept it upstairs someplace because he liked to make me suffer the anxiety of waiting alone in the kitchen while he went upstairs to retrieve it. I would wait with baited breath to endure my fate.

I searched my father's bedroom for its hiding place: under his bed, behind the furniture, everywhere. Then I checked his private dressing room and found the crop leaning against the wall inside his clothes closet. I finally had it. But the newest dilemma for me was that something else had caught my eye as well.

There was a diversion right above it that I had never seen before, and I couldn't keep my eyes—or my hands—off of it. What caught my attention was a leather holster with a silver-plated .38 caliber snub-nosed revolver nestled into it.

Since I was home alone, and I was a curious red-blooded American boy of about eleven years old, I pulled the gun out of the holster and checked it out closely—a little too closely. I'd seen pistols before in Spaghetti Westerns on television, and I toyed with the pistol, pretending that I was going to cock the hammer. Damned if I didn't pull it back too far.

The revolver snapped into firing position. I could see there were bullets in it, and I had just readied the weapon for firing. I didn't know what the heck to do. I was frozen and so scared that for a moment I put the gun in my mouth with my finger on the trigger. I was thinking that my father would kill me for just touching the gun, so I might as well end my misery right then and shoot. I thought no one would care if I lived or died, so what was the difference if I pulled the trigger?

After what seemed like hours standing there, I didn't have the nerve to pull the trigger. I had an idea that I'd try what I had seen in those Westerns, and I put my thumb on the hammer and pulled it back again while slowly squeezing the trigger. I put a finger from my other hand between the hammer and the firing pin, and it actually worked. The gun was no longer cocked. I put the pistol back and ran to my room and hid for the rest of the day. Harrison never found out about that episode, or he might have shot me himself. Actually, it could have fit perfectly into his plan; it could have been his excuse to finally have me committed to the asylum as a danger to myself, the family and society. After all, an eleven-year-old boy playing with a loaded gun definitely fit the bill of an "idiot."

And then there was the infamous "Board of Education." This was a butcher block cutting board about an inch thick with a fat handle. My father liked to use this tool because he could get a good grip on the handle when he spanked us children with it. I found out later that on the rare occasions when he took the other kids into the kitchen to spank them, he would put a phone book or a newspaper over their rear ends so they wouldn't feel it and yet it would still sound like they were getting a beating. Some of them told me later that he would wink at them and whisper for them to scream.

As for me, I got it good with that thing for real. There would be no newspaper or phone book for me, just board on butt. For some reason, Dad loved to dole out his punishment one-on-one in the kitchen; it was certainly his favorite place to educate me. There I was introduced to his "punishment stool." It was a bar stool with metal legs and a plastic seat that sat under a counter in the kitchen. Whenever my father pulled out that stool and I heard the screech of the legs on the tile floor, I had the urge to run and hide. He would make me bend over the stool with my butt in the air and my head near the floor while holding on to its legs. Then he would reach for his Board of Education to teach me my latest painful lesson. It was an ideal prop for Father because the stool was the perfect height for me to bend over and hold onto its steel legs, making my rear end an easy and perfect target.

One day we found that the board mysteriously had the name Harold deeply and perfectly carved into it with a knife. I'm sure it was done by my father, who else would etch my name into the wood and for what reason?

That night I got an especially good beating with it, because after all, it was my name carved into it, and how dare I do something so destructive? My father declared that since it had my name now permanently engraved in it, that I would enjoy the pleasure of its first inaugural schooling. So after the carving incident, the Board of

Education was hung on a wall in the kitchen waiting to be pressed into action. It was forevermore known as Harold's Board of Education, and it was reserved especially for me to earn my master's degree in punishment, pain and penitence.

CHAPTER SEVEN

HOLY BIRTHDAY

It was my thirteenth birthday, and just like any other normal thirteen-year-old boy, I was excited to wake up and celebrate the occasion. Surely my birthday would be something special. I knew we would all share a cake and I'd get a present. I was excited because I would have something new to play with, and I was happy.

For some reason, I always received one small present at my birthday and at Christmas. The Christmas before my birthday, I got a yellow metal Tonka dump truck. I played with that toy for hours on end, and I kept that truck for years, giving it a real workout. I never gave a minute's thought to the fact that my other siblings received many presents, and I got just one. I was just grateful for what I received.

It was a regular weekday morning, and all of us children got up to go to school as usual. Only this wasn't a normal day. My parents sent the three younger siblings to school, and we three older boys were kept home and told to put on our best clothes. Growing up, we always had one pair of dress pants, a shirt and shoes that we were only allowed to wear on special occasions. We wore them so we could dress to impress at the cocktail parties and political events held at the manor.

This day, however, we were to be taken somewhere other than school. Our mother told us we were going to be enrolled at the local Catholic Church. This idea excited me, and I thought was a fantastic birthday present.

As we had never been to a church before, the only thing I knew was that on Sunday, parents and children attended the church down the street in droves. Every Sunday there seemed to be hundreds of families driving by and staring out their car windows at our mansion on their way to attend services. I used to stand on the edge of our property half hidden by the hedges and smile and wave to them as if I were the official greeter at our local tourist attraction of a home. I was thrilled that we were joining because church, in my mind, seemed like the opposite of my secluded and lonely life in the English Manor. I was eager to meet and mingle with all those people who drove by every week.

We were put into the car and driven to downtown Trenton, where we were escorted into an immense and exquisite concrete building with white pillars lining huge concrete stairs that seemed to rise a mile high, higher than I could see. Once we'd climbed those steps, we walked through impressive glass revolving doors and into the grand vestibule of what I thought was a church. It turned out not to be a church at all—it was the Mercer County Courthouse, and it was as grandiose inside as it was on the outside.

The inside was decorated in carved wood. It housed dark wooden pillars and benches, and huge oil paintings of past judges in black robes looked down sternly on the daily activities in the courtroom. A leather-upholstered throne sat atop a platform where the judges looked down and doled out their form of justice.

Two large flags were placed on either side of the chair. One was an American flag, and the other was the flag of the State of New Jersey. As a thirteen-year-old boy who was rarely let out of the house except for school, I was in awe and very intimidated. My jaw dropped seeing this marvelous place, and I don't think my mouth ever closed. I didn't know it, but we were about to meet one of my father's best friends, who was serving as a justice of the Mercer County court system.

We three boys were told to wait in the jury box while my mother and father went into the judge's private chambers. While we were alone, my older brother informed us that there was a man in there who would call us in and ask us some questions. Every question that he asked, we were to say yes and nothing else, not a single word more. I, of course, just had to be different and ask what would happen if I said no. My brother told me the beating I would get when we got home would be like nothing I had gotten before.

Soon a man in what looked like a police uniform came out, and without uttering a word, he ushered us into the judge's chambers. There sat our mother and father along with a man in a black robe perched behind a big wooden desk with a ceiling-to-floor wall of law books behind him.

They had placed three folding chairs for us boys to the side of the desk and in front of our parents, facing them. The judge juggled papers on his desk for a few minutes, and then began a conversation of very few words. The judge looked at my oldest brother and asked him, "Do you understand what we are doing here today and do you agree?" He proudly responded, "Yes, sir."

Then it was the next brother's turn. "Do you understand what we are doing here today and do you agree?" He said, "Yes."

Then came my turn. "Do you understand what we are doing here today and do you agree?" Out again came that little bit of the devil in me, and being a little upset as well as curious—and heck, it was my birthday after all—I didn't answer. You should have seen my parents' panicked and worried looks.

"Do you understand what we are doing here today and do you agree?" asked the judge one more time, this time more forcefully. I hesitated again as, for the first time in my life, I felt some power watching my mother and father squirming in their seats.

I gave in out of fear when I saw my father shaking his head at me menacingly, and I finally muttered a simple, "Yeah." Since they wouldn't tell me what was going on, I wouldn't give them the satisfaction of a "yes," and said "yeah" instead, out of spite.

I never really knew what that day was about, but it didn't feel like joining a church should feel to me. Plus, we never set foot in a church before that day and never after.

Back in the car on the way home, our mom turned around in her seat and said, "Remember, you are now signed up for church, and that's all you say to anyone about this, including your brothers and sister, and that's the end of that!"

The rest of my thirteenth birthday was memorable, too. My parents gave me a basketball for a birthday present. Boy, did I love that ball for the few minutes I had it.

Our mansion was built high on a hill, and as I bounced my new ball for the first time, it hit the tip of my foot and rolled away. It rolled straight down that hill toward the Delaware and Raritan Canal at the end of an alley situated behind our house.

I chased the ball as fast as I could and almost caught up to it, but in it went with a horrific splash. The water in the canal was only about three feet deep, and I wanted to jump in after it, but my father screamed at me, called me an idiot, and made me go home and leave the basketball, which was floating away teasingly just inches from me in a mocking goodbye whirl.

I could easily have followed it down the canal to a bridge over Hermitage Avenue about three blocks away and picked it out of the water with a stick, but my father wouldn't let me. I had to helplessly stand there crying, watching my birthday present drift away. Harrison then beat me for losing my expensive basketball. So some other kid down the street got to enjoy my birthday present, and I got a real birthday spanking.

That day my leg got caught on a screw sticking out of the "punishment stool," and I still have a scar on it from the birthday beating. I always wondered what was so horrible about losing my basketball that I deserved a permanent scar. Wasn't losing my only birthday present within a few seconds of receiving it punishment enough?

Or was it that I was a little too cocky signing up for church that morning? Maybe I took too long to answer, and maybe they didn't like that I said "yeah" instead of a hearty "yes, sir."

So happy thirteenth birthday to me, signed up for church, lost my ball, and got a beating to boot, none of which made any sense to me at all.

CHAPTER EIGHT

NINE-MONTH PAROLE

In the spring of 1969, I turned seventeen years old, and I was more than ready to grasp my independence. My father became severely sick that summer with recurring bouts of nausea, and as a trained medical doctor, he treated himself for weeks as though it were a simple flu. This treatment turned out to be fruitless, as his illness was something far more serious. He had contracted cancer of the stomach.

He fought it hard through nine months of treatment at the Hospital of the University of Pennsylvania. As a renowned psychiatrist, he was afforded the luxury very few of us receive. He was given a private hospital room where my mother stayed in the bed next to him for most of the nine months he was a patient. The doctors in Philly treated him with an experimental drug that the experts thought might save his life, but it prolonged the inevitable, and he died a horribly slow and painful death.

During those nine months, his body seemed to melt away until he looked like a living skeleton. Near the end of his life, my father was so thin that I could see his bones protruding through his skin.

The hospital room had a pungent odor that has stayed with me to this day. When visiting on Saturdays, we kids would sit in his room quietly. No one would say a word. There was nothing we could do except sit and stare at this once strong man, now too weak to sip from his water cup without assistance. My brothers and sister and I would make up excuses to leave the room—anything to get out of there. Either we had to go to the bathroom or we were thirsty and needed a drink. We did whatever we could to avoid sitting there in morbid silence for hours on end watching the final curtain fall on Harrison Force English.

In his last days, he didn't seem to recognize anyone, and he could only manage an empty stare and a weak muffled response.

None of the children wanted to be alone in the English Manor during the time our parents were in Philadelphia at the hospital. We weren't told anything about the illness, so we didn't comprehend the seriousness of what was going on. We went about our lives and stayed away from the house and each other as much as we could.

We looked for any reason to avoid contact with each other and, thus, the dreaded conversation. My brothers and sister would disappear somewhere in the English Manor or stay at a friend's house as much as they could.

Having no friends, I would come home from school and jump onto my Schwinn bicycle and ride for hours through Cadwalader Park. That one-speed red bike with a brown and white seat and a silver bell on the handlebars was the only means of freedom I had ever known. I would ride alone with the wind, wondering what the heck was going on with my family, the world, and more particularly, my father.

The park was a great escape for me, and it also became my salvation. High on a hill in the center of the park stood the Monkey House, which once had been the home of the original owner of the parklands. It had been remodeled and fitted with cages to house the monkeys, and it normally displayed a dozen or so primates for any spectators who could brave the stench to feed them peanuts and watch them perform.

A couple of bear cages had been built into the side of a small hill nearby. Park visitors could walk on a grate over the tops of the cages and look down and feed the bears. There was also a petting zoo filled with deer, sheep, peacocks, and other animals.

My favorite hangout was the small amusement park sitting at the edge of the Delaware and Raritan Canal. It housed a carousel complete with the usual miniature fire trucks, trains, and elephants on which to ride round and round. The park also had the prerequisite swings and seesaws, even a little pool with boat rides.

I would lean my bike against a tree and sit on a park bench for hours enviously watching parents and children playing, laughing and enjoying each other. Cotton candy, peanuts, balloons, and rides for everyone.

On weekends a balloon man stationed himself at the main entrance to the park, and parents lined up in droves with their eager children to pick out the perfect balloon to top off their adventures and help them remember their great day at the park.

This is the way I dreamed that life should be for everyone. This is the way I wanted life to be with all of my heart. All was right with the world while I was in Cadwalader Park; all was wrong with my world directly across the street in the English Manor.

As horrible as my father's excruciatingly slow death was, those nine months were an incredible, lifesaving gift to me, a true godsend. With both him and my mother away in Philadelphia, I took a little freedom for the first time in my life. I left the confines of the manor and ventured into the world to make some friends in the neighborhood.

Hatrack's, a drugstore a few blocks away from our house at the corner of Stuyvesant and Hoffman avenues, seemed always to be abuzz with activity. I started walking back and forth in front of it every day just to watch people. A group of neighborhood kids used to hang out every afternoon in front of Hatrack's, and meeting them was like discovering a new family and a whole new life. I quickly became an accepted member of their group, and I looked forward to hanging out in front of the drugstore with my new family.

On that street corner was where I met my best friend, Jap. His real name was Chris, and he was a true badass. He was a few years older, and most other kids were afraid of him because he seemed a little bit crazy. If anyone gave him an attitude, he would get into their face with a mad dog stare until they had to look away.

Since he was older, Jap would go across the street to the liquor store and buy a few quarts of beer for us to drink while hanging out. His preferred brand was Schlitz, and it came in a cardboard quart container. The liquor store would pour draft beer right into the white cylindrical container and then top it with a round lid, making it easier for us to dump if the cops came around.

Jap wasn't muscular, but he had no fear of anyone because he was a black belt in karate. He was the true leader of the pack, a James Dean kind of guy. He was six foot two inches tall with a thin, athletic physique, and he was a really good-looking kid. He had light brown hair, a toothy smile, and two big dimples.

Jap loved nice clothes and looked great in all of his many hats. Mostly he wore one of those Irish paperboy-type flat caps, but other times, a baseball cap or a Navy skull cap would complete his outfit. Jap always coordinated his clothes and hats, and he had about a half-dozen pair of Converse sneakers in different colors to match perfectly with the rest of his outfits.

All of the neighborhood girls loved Jap, and they would whisper, giggle or mumble things to their girlfriends as he walked past them on the street. It was Jap who set me up on my first date. We double-dated with a couple of girls in Trenton's predominantly Jewish neighborhood called Hiltonia. The Hiltonia section was a short walk through Cadwalader Park on the opposite side of the park from the English Manor.

It really wasn't much of a date, but it was the first time I was alone with a girl. Jap and I got dressed in our best jeans and dress shirts. I slapped on a generous dose of my brother's Brut cologne, and Jap put on a splash of his Old English Leather aftershave. We strolled to Hiltonia, where Jap's date was babysitting with her friend, who was my blind date for the evening. With my date's parents out for the night and her younger brother already in bed, we all sat around and ate popcorn and started watching a movie on television.

It wasn't long before Jap stood up and took his girl by the hand, and they both went upstairs to "check on the kid." They were gone for a long time while I sat quietly watching the movie. I had rarely been out of the house, let alone on a date, so I had no idea that I was supposed to make out with my girl. I also had no clue why Jap and his date hadn't come back. I just remember repeating, "I wonder where they are?" My date just looked at me like I was crazy and slowly shook her head in dismay. All we did was watch the movie until Jap came downstairs, and then we left. Jap kissed his girl goodnight while I shook my date's hand. I thought I was being the perfect gentleman that night, but needless to say, she didn't want to go out with me ever again. And Jap? Well, he couldn't stop laughing at me the whole walk home.

Jap was tough, and he was not afraid of anything. As we grew closer, I realized that he was as smart as anyone but that he purposely hid it. I think he felt that if anyone knew he was smart, he would lose his tough-guy mystique. I learned a lot about life on the streets from Jap during the short time we had together as best friends.

Everyone in our street gang had a nickname, and I loved it. Jap got his because he loved old Japanese war movies, had a Samurai sword hanging over his bed, and was always practicing his karate moves, swiping at the air and making noises.

Stubby was a short, tough kid who always carried a chip on his shoulder as if he had something to prove, and he was always looking for a fight. He would pick a fight at the drop of a hat and sometimes even no hat. George the Greek drove a 1963 Ford Galaxie. Irish Murf, a tall, obviously Irish kid, was a couple years older than the rest of us. He had a job, an apartment, a girlfriend, and a car, and that made him a very cool guy. Johnny Money was about the same age as my oldest brother, and he was a very mellow guy. Nothing bothered him, and he never bothered anyone. Money's father had died a few years before we met, and he had inherited his dad's car. It was a beautiful gray 1963 Cadillac Coupe De Ville. Sweet ride!

Johnny never had a job and was always high from smoking marijuana. He used to cruise around the neighborhood in that big Cadillac all day long puffing on a joint. I loved riding shotgun with him and blasting his eight-track tapes.

Stubby introduced me to Linda, who was my first crush. She was absolutely beautiful. A nice, shy neighborhood girl, she had long black hair, big brown eyes, and beautiful dark skin. Linda allowed me my very first kiss. I never got to second base with her because she was more introverted than I was. But life has a funny way of changing us, because years later she was arrested for prostitution at a local shopping center. She'd made the mistake of soliciting a cop who was walking out of a delicatessen after buying his lunch.

And then there was my buddy Herc. He was nicknamed after Hercules, not because he was a strong muscleman, but because he loved the television show. Herc, a tall and skinny kid, was very nice but dumb as a post. His claim to fame in the neighborhood was that his mother had once stabbed him in the shoulder with a fork for mouthing off to her at dinner. Jap and I took him to my house that night and patched him up with gauze and tape. And I'd thought my mom was nuts.

Jap and I hung out together every day and night for most of the nine months that my father was away. Jap would come to my house or I would go to his, and then we would walk to the corner drugstore, where we would hang out with the other guys and drink Jap's beer. There was a restaurant near the corner called the Roly Poly, and I got my first job there making pizza, a skill that was useful in later years.

Jap and I got high a lot. His older brother was in the Navy, and he and his friends provided us with a steady supply of marijuana and hashish. Jap said the soldiers flew it to America from Vietnam inside the tires of military airplanes. Then the military mechanics took it out and sold it, splitting the profits.

I once took a drive with Jap to Seaside Heights, a small New Jersey seashore town. We were only there for about an hour, as he said he had a quick errand to run. We went on the boardwalk and he placed a couple of twenty dollar bills on a spinning wheel game. His number didn't win, but the guy behind the booth, who wore a military cap with Vietnam patches all over it, shouted, "Winner! Winner!" and gave Jap a carton of cigarettes. We left immediately, driving home with the carton. At home he opened a pack and lit a cigarette. The tobacco had been removed, and it was now packed with marijuana.

Our gang never bothered anybody, but man, if anybody bothered one of us, they would get their butts kicked. One day that summer a gang from a few blocks away beat up Herc for just walking down a street nearby called Hermitage Avenue, their so-called turf. They proudly called themselves the Hermitage Mafia. The next night a bunch of us headed over to Hermitage Avenue and beat the heck out of a couple of the Hermitage Mafia guys. The rest of them ran like the wind while we chased them and warned them that if they showed up in our neighborhood they would be dead. We never saw them after that, and no one bothered any of us again. It felt great to be under the protection of my new family.

One Sunday afternoon, Jap came to my house and pulled a small, square piece of paper out of his pocket and held it up for me to see. It was a plain white scrap of paper about an inch square with a pink dot in the middle. He said it was paper acid (LSD) and that we could take a cool trip on it. I guess curiosity got the better of us, and we decided to do it.

Jap tore the paper tab in half so we were sure we would each get only a half-dose. After all, how could half of it hurt us? We each placed our half of the paper tab onto our tongues in anticipation of a great high and just stood there while it melted in our mouths.

We went on a trip, all right. In about ten minutes, everything looked like it does when characters hallucinate in the movies. People looked like cartoons of themselves. Everyone we saw had huge, swollen heads and small bodies. It was hysterical. I thought I was laughing for hours, but it might have been only a few minutes. We had a hard time keeping track of time, and we really didn't care. We left the confines of my house and wandered around in a stupor in the safety of Cadwalader Park.

As I walked, I felt as though I wasn't using my own feet and legs but those of someone else. I couldn't feel my limbs. I seemed to be the starring character of a cartoon, and everything that we saw or did seemed comical and made me laugh.

Some of our friends were in the park playing a pickup game of football, and it was one of the funniest things I had ever seen. When they threw the ball, it looked as though it were in slow motion. When they jumped to catch the ball, I thought they were floating. Their eyes seemed to pop out of their faces when they strained to catch it. I could hear every grunt and every breath from afar. My hearing seemed magnified, yet somehow every sound was muffled.

The cartoon I was in seemed to take over my voice and numb my tongue. My voice sounded high-pitched and garbled to me. I could feel drool seeping out of the corner of my mouth as though I were in a dentist's chair pumped full of Novocain, but I didn't care. My body was throbbing, but I was in another world and couldn't feel much of anything. Distant sounds whizzed past my ears. Car horns blared out long and slow. Dogs barked, children played, all muffled and in slow motion. Everything seemed far, far away, as though I was viewing it from inside a tunnel, and the scenes caused me to laugh and laugh.

Jap and I sat under a tree while our friends kept coming close to us making funny faces. "Are you guys okay?" they asked. They were looking into our eyes while shaking their heads and mumbling, "You guys are messed up."

That afternoon I earned my nickname, Happy. They called me Happy because I always walked around with a grin on my face. Who wouldn't be happy getting out of the prison I'd grown up in and discovering a great big world full of wonderful things and interesting people, all of whom accepted me as an equal?

A few days after that LSD trip, I went to Jap's house to hang out as usual. Jap's parents answered the door together and told me he couldn't come out because he was sick. When I asked what was wrong and whether I could get him anything, his parents ushered me into their living room and had me sit on the couch. They kept looking at each other to see which one of them was going to give me the bad news.

After a few awkward moments his mom finally said, "He's not that kind of sick." She choked up as she spoke. "Chris is mentally ill and was taken to and admitted into the Trenton Psychiatric Hospital a few hours ago."

I felt a rush of cold liquid moving through my veins, and my face burned bright red. I was in shock. After what seemed like hours of dead silence, but more likely was only a few minutes, I stood up and left the house. As hard as I tried, I couldn't find the right words—or any words at all—to say to Jap's parents.

Earlier that morning, the Trenton police had found Jap walking along the railroad tracks near his house. He was slicing weird symbols into his arms with a razor blade and mumbling incoherently. They knew Jap from the corner gang and took him home, but he didn't recognize anyone, so with his parents' permission, the police took him to the Trenton Psychiatric Hospital for testing.

I've always wondered if maybe Jap never really came down off of that trip we took. The LSD, plus the fact that he was a little crazy to begin with, could have been too much for him to handle.

A few days after getting the bad news about Jap, my friends and I decided to visit him at the hospital. We were sure that when he saw us, we could snap him out of it and get him out of that crazy place.

When we arrived at the hospital, we had to stop at a security checkpoint upon turning off the road onto the asylum grounds. Security was housed in a large stone building with chicken wire and bars blocking its windows, which were covered with that damn creeping ivy. Once security got our names and the license plate of Johnny's Cadillac, we were told to drive to the main building and check in.

Driving up the long, winding, tree-lined driveway of the Trenton Madhouse gave me a creepy feeling. The trees were hundred-year-old majestic oaks with branches arching over the road, forming a tunnel underneath. Even in the daylight, it was dark in this nature-made passageway, and as bright as the sun was, it couldn't sneak a peek through the thick leaves. The car radio kept changing stations between "In-A-Gadda-Da-Vida" by Iron Butterfly and some polka station—creepy. I was riding in my usual shotgun position, and I reached over to shut it off, leaving us in eerie silence.

Despite my father having been a top psychiatrist of the hospital, I had never actually seen it, so I didn't know what to expect. The closer we got to the building, the more I started to sweat and the harder it got to breathe. I was afraid to tell any of the staff at the hospital my name for fear something would happen to me, so I used a fake name at security.

As Johnny Money's Cadillac drove farther onto the grounds, we could see a large and imposing, castle-like building with a huge dome in the middle of its roof, surrounded by a group of smaller buildings. It was a magnificent throwback to the Victorian era, and it immediately looked and felt haunted to us. The grounds of the hospital were extensive.

People were scattered about outside with rakes and shovels, performing general landscaping duties. We figured most of them were probably patients because of the jumpsuits and canvas shoes they wore. They all had dazed looks on their faces and paid attention to nothing and to no one. We assumed the hospital allowed the less dangerous patients to work outside for therapy and exercise.

Making our way around the circular drive in front of the main building, we could see some other similar buildings. Many were much smaller, with signs posted in front announcing their function. The labels on the buildings included Power House, Green House, Laundry, Cafeteria, Store House, and Trading Post. One building was labeled Police, and one was called the Warden's House.

It seemed like this asylum was an isolated and self-contained world unto itself. We all came to the realization that no one needed to leave the grounds for any reason, and all at once we grasped that this was less like a hospital and more like a prison, warden and all. We started to feel claustrophobic and nervous.

As we entered the administration building, it felt like we had entered a different realm. It was quiet and unnerving. A heavy smell of industrial chemicals permeated the air. We had to sign in again with security. I had to attest that Jap was my brother so we could get in to see him, because the rules that were boldly posted on the wall said that only family was allowed to visit.

We were ushered by security on a twenty-minute journey through the many tunnels and narrow hallways of the asylum. We walked through several locked doors that the guards had to unlock, let us through, and then lock again behind us, a very somber experience.

After what seemed like forever, we reached the ward where Jap was housed. As we entered, we passed many patients wandering around the place aimlessly and unescorted.

Since we were being escorted by a security guard, I asked him why so many patients were wandering around alone. The guard told us they were heavily medicated and that there was no danger of them becoming violent, so they were free to stroll around the ward. He told us some of them were incarcerated there because there was no room in the regular prisons.

We noticed that all of the patients seemed to have one thing in common: bleary, dilated eyes. The hallways were relatively quiet except for an unnerving, sporadic scream or moan from a patient in the distance. We all flinched or jumped whenever we heard one of those low moans. Closely passing a couple of the permanent residents of the madhouse, we could see directly into their eyes, and we all agreed they looked like zombies.

I couldn't help but wonder if the heavy medication was just prolonging their stay at the asylum and not curing them at all. It seemed to me that these patients had no chance of recovery while they were heavily doped up, but what did I know? I wasn't the psychiatrist, my father was. I had a terrible feeling that my best friend Jap was in very big and very serious trouble.

When we arrived at Jap's room, it was empty except for a small cot, a table, and my best friend. It was evident that it wasn't a normal hospital room but a sterile jail cell. We had brought Jap a couple of cartons of Lucky Strike cigarettes, which turned out to be a good call. Cigarettes were a sort of currency inside the asylum. Patients swapped them for clean socks, extra food or snacks, and even drugs. Some of the patients played poker most of the day, using their cigarettes as cash. We had inadvertently staked Jap to a poker game.

Jap was still out of it and didn't recognize any of us during the visit, not even me. He seemed lost to another world. He was in his own parallel existence, and no matter how hard we tried, we couldn't bring him back. It felt to me as though he didn't want to come back to reality and preferred to stay in this new world where he had taken up residence. The whole time we were there, he just complained to us that he needed more socks. That's all he kept saying over and over—that the other inmates were stealing his socks. He kept talking to himself as if we weren't in the cell with him. It was the saddest and scariest thing I have ever witnessed.

Even though he didn't know who we were, we all promised him we would be back with socks and more cigarettes, and we shouted for the guard to let us out.

We took the long, solemn walk out of the complex in silence. It wasn't until we got into the car and drove off the grounds that we started talking about all the misery that place had seen and had probably caused over the years. We could feel the horror and suffering seeping through the ivy walls of that sad place. I took a lot of crap from the guys that day because my father had worked in this creepy madhouse, but I think they finally realized that I wasn't the spoiled rich kid they'd first thought I was. I was actually one of them, just a regular kid from the streets.

After a couple more visits to Jap, I couldn't bring myself to go in that place anymore. I was a stranger to him, and he didn't remember I'd been there from one visit to the next. I couldn't take the sadness anymore. Jap just kept repeating the same things over and over. I wondered how he could have slipped so far from reality so fast. I kept thinking about all the patients living so closely together, side by side, each in their own dimension, each in their own universe. The only positive thing I could think of was that they were so drugged they couldn't possibly be feeling any pain, and Jap had always loved being high.

I never saw or heard anything about Jap after that last lonely visit. Forty years later, I ran into an old friend from the neighborhood. It turned out she'd been working at the psychiatric hospital for the past twenty years. She told me that Jap had died a few weeks before. He was under psychiatric care for more than thirty-five years, and Jap had never regained his sanity. He was heavily medicated the entire time and in no pain. She said that he—not much of a poker player—had never had any cigarettes or socks. I wish I could have sent him a supply every month for those thirty-five years; I would feel a whole lot better about it today.

I do take some comfort knowing that Jap was high the whole time, and I know he was always the happiest when he was on a high. The State of New Jersey provided him with only the best of drugs for the rest of his life.

It's even sadder to me when I realize Jap was quite brilliant and was possibly one of the smartest people I have ever known. I believe he could have been someone special, and he could have made a positive impact on this world. I think of Jap often, and I sometimes wonder what would have happened to me if he had handed me his half of that LSD tab instead of mine. It's so hard to deal with the fact that such a brilliant mind slipped away from this world, never to return. Rest in peace Jap, my best friend.

CHAPTER NINE

FATHER'S GONE

I was seventeen years old in January of 1970 when my mother finally came home from the hospital in Philadelphia late one cold winter night. She had my older brother call us all down from our bedrooms to gather in the living room, where she was sitting in her usual seat under Harrison's oil portrait. It was hard to get the younger children out of bed in the middle of the night.

When all six kids were in the living room, my mother simply said, "I guess you all know why we're here. Your father died today." Then she broke down crying.

After her solemn announcement, there was a pregnant pause for few moments that seemed like an eternity. None of us reacted or spoke. We just sat and stared at each other in confused silence, trying to process the news and figure out what we were supposed to do now.

We'd all been brought up to be "seen and not heard," so none of us knew how to express our opinions or our feelings about his death. We were always taught to be non-communicators, and we couldn't find any words. The harsh reality is that I have never spoken to any of the other children about our father's life or death since that night. We each retreated into our own rooms, our own worlds, and the torture of our own thoughts.

I went to my bedroom and I vomited. I don't know why I had that reaction to the news. I felt horrible because that night I realized that I had never loved my father—I had never had any feelings other than fear and hatred for him—and it took his death to make me realize it.

I just didn't get it. How could I not love my father? Even after all the years of abuse, how could that be? I wondered what was wrong with me. I had many tortured thoughts that sleepless night that maybe my father had been right about me all along—maybe I was a wicked person, and maybe I was truly an idiot as he'd always said. I couldn't get a grip on my lack of feelings for him.

Instead of the grief that I should have felt, I was upset with my father for passing away. I was angry with him for dying so early, before I grew big enough to punch him in the mouth for all he had done to me over the years.

As I lay in bed that night, I desperately wanted to pay him back for the mental abuse and the beatings he'd given me, and he had robbed me of any chance of retaliation. He had ruined my fantasy of one day standing up to him, taking that riding crop out of his hands and whipping him with it. That fantasy of sweet revenge was the only thing that had gotten me through some of the punishment he'd doled out. I would bend over that punishment stool and mentally reverse roles, dreaming that I was the one hitting him. My father had just died, and yet my only two emotions were deep relief and the sense that I'd been cheated out of my right to retribution. I was one messed-up kid, just like my father had always said, and it took his death for me to finally realize that he'd been right about me all along.

That night, the night of Harrison's death, was the last time I remember the six English children alone together in the same room with Mom.

During those nine months while my parents were at the hospital in Philadelphia, one of my brothers was placed in charge and supposedly was taking care of us children. My brother seemed to me to want to show off his newfound power and prove that he was now the rightful lord and master of the English Manor.

One afternoon while we were both in the kitchen, he pushed a dirty frying pan into my gut as hard as he could, thus he knocked a little wind out of me. He barked, "Clean that pan and cook my lunch!" I somehow found an inner strength that I had never experienced before. I told him there were other frying pans that were clean, and that if he wanted to use that one, he should clean it himself because I wasn't his maid, and by the way, he should cook his own lunch, as I wasn't his personal chef, either.

I couldn't believe that I had actually spoken up for myself for the first time in my life. It felt empowering.

My brother was shocked that I had spoken back, and he seemed a little embarrassed. He screamed at me, "You wash it right now, or else!" Then, when my head was turned away from him, he sucker punched me in the face, right under my eye. The stones on a ring he was wearing cut my face, and it started bleeding profusely. Once I took my hand away and saw the blood, I went nuts. I punched him in the jaw, knocking him against the kitchen counter. He looked shocked, and he was fuming that I had dared to raise a hand to him. He kept coming after me, taking random swings like a madman.

Not one of his punches landed, as I was backing away from him with my hands in the air, blocking the shots. My younger brother yelled at him to stop, screaming that I was grown up and too big for him to handle, and that I could hurt him.

I think hearing that statement from my younger brother was all the encouragement I needed. I reached out and grabbed hold of the little beard my older brother was sporting on his chin, hauled back my arm, and punched him in the face as hard as I could. I was amazed when he spun around and his upper body flipped over my infamous "punishment stool." My hand felt like it had broken, but it was the best pain I had ever felt. It felt amazing. It wasn't Harrison giving me a beating anymore; now I was beating somebody else against that kitchen stool.

I didn't know how to feel about my little brother stepping into the fight. He had instinctively given me the first words of encouragement in my seventeen years of life. It empowered me, and I had a triumphant feeling of independence.

After the fight, I left the house and walked around Cadwalader Park for hours, finally returning to the house later that night. My brother pulled me aside and apologized for his behavior. He said he was sorry he'd acted that way. All I said in response was, "Hey, we're all kids and we're all under a lot of pressure, no problem."

But it was a problem for me—a major problem. I didn't trust him, and I was scared. I felt that my brother would pay me back somehow, some way, maybe even in my sleep. I felt that as long as we lived in the same house, I would never be safe. I was a mess of feelings that night, and the only thing I was sure of was that no one was going to put their hands on me or abuse me again, ever.

Shortly after my father died, my friends Murf, Herc, Johnny and George, along with a couple of other guys, took me to a neighborhood apartment. I didn't know who the person who lived there was, but the apartment was on the second floor of an old Victorian house, and it was a sort of hippie place.

Our host's hair was in a ponytail reaching down to his belt, and he wore worn-out bell bottom jeans ripped in several spots. He sported a tie dyed T-shirt, sandals, beads around his neck, and a beaded band around his head. He called the place his "crib." Rows of colored plastic beads hung from the door frames, and a tapestry that covered one whole living room wall looked as though it might have been an Oriental rug. A poster hung over the stereo of the Beatles' *Sergeant Pepper's Lonely Hearts Club Band.*

On the center of the coffee table—really just an old wooden orange crate—stood a Hookah pipe that had wine in it instead of water and four long hoses coming out of it. It was being used for smoking hashish. A shelf on the wall housed an awesome sounding Pioneer stereo system that had a turntable under a glass dust cover, large speakers, and an eight-track tape player. A whole bookshelf was filled with hundreds of record albums and eight-track tapes. That music sounded pretty good, but it got even better as the night went on.

My friends lit up some marijuana, put on a Jimmy Hendrix album and starting passing around the joint. After a little while they lit another joint, and then another. We were passing it around the room while sitting on the floor and playing some of the best music I had ever heard. Being sheltered and kept in the house all those years, I'd never had a record player or a radio, and it was the first time I had ever heard the Beatles, Jimmy Hendrix, the Rolling Stones, Cream, Steppenwolf or Bob Dylan on a real stereo rather than a crackly one-speaker car radio. My favorite—and last—song that I heard that night was "Whiter Shade of Pale" by a group called

Procol Harum. I felt as though I was right there on stage with the musicians.

I didn't realize at the time what my friends were doing, but after smoking the first joint, they all faked it and stopped taking hits. They let me smoke and smoke until I was so high that I actually passed out. I was drifting, floating out of my body and dreaming. I dreamed that the ivy covering the English Manor walls was wilting and rotting away and that the stone walls were disintegrating into dust. I dreamed of what life would be like from now on, on my own without my father's abuse.

The next morning when I woke up, I knew what I had to do. I had to leave home and go away to start a new life for myself. I had sampled a little taste of independence and happiness, and I had become addicted to them both—I had to have more. I just couldn't take any more negativity in my life, and I knew I had to find another place that was both physically and emotionally healthier. I came to the sobering realization that I had to grow up and become a man, and I had to do it then and there.

A few weeks later, I left home. It wasn't planned, and I didn't have a job or a place to live, but I left. At that time, I was living in fear of what my brother planned as revenge for me punching him and humiliating him. He sported the black eye I gave him for several weeks, and he was embarrassed about it. I also felt guilt as one of six kids living off a widowed mother who had no visible means of support, and I didn't want that on my conscience. Eating her food and being a financial burden played heavily into my rash decision. It didn't occur to me that none of the other children may have felt the same way. I did, and that's all I cared about.

Fortunately for me it was springtime when I left home, because I didn't plan my escape very well. One day I had just had enough of this life, and I left home with nothing but the T-shirt on my back, a pair of blue jeans, a denim jacket, and my Converse sneakers. I just walked away. Back in the late 1960s the term homeless wasn't in common use, so I was considered a bum or vagabond.

I had no money, nothing of value, no confidence or self-esteem, no sense of self-worth. I just had a wild and crazy dream of happiness and independence.

My first couple of nights that I spent homeless was uneventful. The weather was beautiful with clear skies and plenty of stars lighting my way. I thought the best place to sleep where I would not disturb anyone and would not be bothered by anyone would be a few blocks from the house along the banks of the Delaware River.

Unfortunately for Trenton, its industry and its housing were built facing away from the Delaware River. All of the buildings turned their backs on what should have been the city's greatest natural resource, the river. That made it almost impossible to reach the water by car in most places, rendering the area abandoned at night.

Years before, a highway, Route 29, had been built right over the top of a canal that flowed parallel to the river just one hundred feet away. Towns farther to the north and south of Trenton had used this canal as a tow path. Barges were towed up and down the canal by mules to get goods back and forth in the early days, and now the canal was used as a tourist attraction. By building the highway, Trenton had caused the river to be blocked off from the city and had created a man-made buffer between the river and the highway. This spot seemed to be the perfect place to hide at night. I was sure I would be safe and could get some undisturbed rest there.

Exploring the banks of the Delaware, I found an old concrete foundation that had held up a bridge destroyed by major floods years before. The bridge spanned the Delaware River between Trenton and Morrisville, Pennsylvania. I had a few peaceful and uneventful nights nestled under and in between a couple of large, broken slabs of concrete. It was the perfect spot for protection from the weather and for the privacy I needed. It turned out that I needed protection from more than just the elements, but I hadn't realized it yet.

In the middle of my third night, I was rudely awakened from a deep sleep. I was dreaming that I was running. I just kept running and running. In my dream, I wasn't sure if someone was chasing me or if I was running toward someone or something, I just knew that I had to run.

Then I felt a tingling sensation in my legs. This graduated into pain, and it went on for what seemed like a very long time. In my dream, I thought I was experiencing cramps from running. The pain finally got so unbearable that it woke me up.

I looked down at my legs in the dark, with only the light from the moon. When my eyes adjusted to the dark, I saw what looked like a half-dozen cats licking my legs. As my eyes adjusted and began to focus, I realized that they weren't cats. They were river rats.

The rats were as big as cats and looked like they might have weighed ten pounds each. Fortunately, they had just started licking at my legs when I awoke and scared them off. I don't know who was more scared, me or the rats, but at least they scattered before biting into me.

I later learned that there were hundreds of these cat-like rodents living on and around the riverbank. They would swim in the river all day, and that bridge foundation turned out to be their favorite place to sleep at night, as well as mine. I was trespassing in their home and they were welcoming me ... as dinner.

I never went back to spend the night at the river again. I was too scared to sleep there, although I did find it to be a great spot to wash myself in the mornings.

For the next several months, I slept in Cadwalader Park under the trees and bushes. It was the best and most peaceful sleep I'd ever had. I washed myself in the mornings as best as I could in either the river or the bathroom of a gas station up the street. My friends fed me once in a while by sneaking snacks from their homes for me. I didn't realize it then, but I must have been quite a sight, as I didn't even own a comb and my hair had grown down to my shoulders. It had gotten so bad that it was matted at one time and I sported a poor dirty version of dreadlocks.

As this was my senior year in high school, I had no choice but to drop out. Living in the same clothes every day and being unable to get completely clean was not conducive to high school success. I slept in the park near the school bus stop and was awakened every morning by the sounds of the high school kids waiting for and then getting onto the school bus, laughing and joking with each other without a care in the world.

My day started as the school bus rolled away full of children who had a future, unlike me. Then I walked the neighborhood all day looking for something to eat, something to do, and someone to do it with.

There was a wonderful bakery in the neighborhood, owned by an elderly German couple who did all the baking themselves. They had no children but were kind to the local kids.

One day shortly after I left home, I was walking through an alleyway behind the bakery, keeping an eye out for a good place to sleep. As I passed the back door of the bakery, I spotted the baker putting his daily trash into a garbage can. One man's garbage is another man's treasure, and I could not believe my luck. He was throwing out what turned out to be my salvation.

He was tossing out broken pastries, day-old donuts, and breads that he couldn't sell in the bakery. I had hit the culinary jackpot, the mother lode of gastronomical delights. Later that night I came back to the alley and feasted on pieces of broken lemon meltaways, raisin biscuits, cream and jelly donuts, apple strudel, breads, cookies ... I ate until I couldn't put another morsel into my mouth. I took two pieces of day-old rye bread, crushed a jelly donut between them, and had my first sandwich in a long time.

That garbage can was the most magnificent smorgasbord that I had ever seen. I had found myself a steady supply of food, and as non-nutritious as it was, I was saved. To this day I have never been able to find a lemon meltaway as delicious as those that I dug out of the trash can.

After several nights of dining at what I called Ye Olde Pastry Shoppe Waste Receptacle, I was caught red-handed by the baker and his wife. One evening they were working late and both of them came out of the back of the bakery, catching me with a mouth full of cookies. The wife screamed, "What are you doing!?" and I thought I would be going to jail. They asked me very sternly what I was doing there, and when I told them the truth—that I was homeless and hungry—the baker and his wife took pity on me.

The baker made a deal with me that if I came every day at three o'clock in the afternoon and swept the floor, I could leave with a little white paper bag filled with whatever baked goods I could fit into it. When I said I would love to do that, the baker took me inside and handed me a broom and a white bakery bag to fill when I was finished sweeping.

I never ate out of a garbage can again. I was now happily sweeping flour off of that bakery's wooden floor and filling a white bag with pastries every day. What a stark contrast between this chore and scraping dog crap off the concrete floor at the English Manor and filling that brown paper grocery bag with those nasty droppings.

Another saving grace during my homeless days was Gino's Hamburgers. Gino's was across town on South Broad Street. It was owned by Gino Marchetti, a former football player with the Baltimore Colts. My friend Johnny Money had a younger cousin who worked the night shift there on Fridays and Saturdays.

Johnny and I would pick him up and drive him home after his shift ended. At eleven o'clock each night, his cousin would cook up a bunch of burgers and fries that he knew they would never sell before closing time. Gino's had a policy that employees could take home any leftover food that was cooked and had not been sold so they didn't have to throw it out. Johnny's cousin would jump in the car with a couple bags of chicken, burgers and fries, and we would pig out while driving him home. My weekdays were spent eating fresh baked goods, and on weekends I munched on free chicken, burgers and fries. Life was now good!

Two of my older friends from the neighborhood had cars, and they would leave them unlocked so I could sleep in the back seat once in a while if the weather was inclement. These accommodations were much nicer than under a tree. It was a luxury having a car roof over my head and a padded seat to sleep on—to me, it was like being in a plush hotel. That is, until the local police got wise to me and drove around the neighborhood looking for me every night.

The constabulary loved to find me, bang their nightsticks on the car window, and order me to go home. I never understood why they bothered with me, but I realized there wasn't much crime in the neighborhood, so they had nothing better to do but search for me and roust me. It must have broken the monotony of their night shifts to play their newest game, "Where's Harold?"

One night when they found me sound asleep in the backseat of George the Greek's Ford Galaxie, they did more than just wake me up and tell me to go home. For some reason, they decided to tear apart the car searching for drugs. I guess I did look like a druggie.

It was about midnight, and they made me lean against a tree while they radioed to another police car, which pulled up with sirens blaring and lights flashing. By this time there was an audience of neighbors, including George's parents, gathered in robes and pajamas. It was humiliating standing there looking like a criminal while they searched the car, even taking out the back seat and throwing it onto the ground. I just kept looking at George's parents, who were shooting angry looks at their son for allowing me to sleep in his car.

The cops found what they were looking for—drugs. A single pill had fallen behind the seat where I'd been sleeping. The officer who found it acted like a giddy teenager, holding up this dangerous pharmaceutical for all the neighbors to see. He probably was fantasizing about a big promotion for his first major drug bust, thinking he might even get his picture in the newspaper. The senior officer walked over, took one look at the pill, and pronounced that it was a false alarm. The dangerous drug was simply an aspirin that someone had dropped behind the seat.

The neighbors laughed at the officer while shaking their heads and walking back to their homes, and the embarrassed rookie cop who'd discovered the pill ordered me to turn around and assume the position. I had to submit to his patting me down while I leaned against the tree, and he even made me take off my sneakers and socks. Finding nothing, he threw my Converses at me and commanded me to get out of his sight and go home.

Never did I go home again. There was no going home, because there really was no home for me. Whenever the cops rousted me, I would simply walk around the corner and disappear. I would just find another place to sleep, under a tree or somewhere, anywhere they wouldn't find me. I wasn't ever going home.

I later got good at locating hiding spots, and I'd sneak onto people's front porches late at night and sleep on their porch furniture. When the morning paperboy threw the newspaper on the porch, it would wake me up and I'd leave before anyone was the wiser.

My porch-hopping worked for weeks, and I was only caught once, by Johnny Money's mom. She punished me by making me come in and have a breakfast of scrambled eggs, rye toast, bacon and orange juice with her before she went to work. What a sweetheart she was. That was my first home-cooked meal in months, and she knew it but never said a word.

After a while, the cops didn't hassle me anymore. Maybe they gave up because I wasn't bothering anybody and I was now on private property, or maybe they just tired of the game and knew I wasn't giving up and going home, ever.

CHAPTER TEN

IT'S ONLY A NAME

After leaving home and coming to the realization that I was finally a free and independent person, I knew I had to make a major decision. Deep in the recesses of my mind, I felt that I had to become a different person than Harold, the unwanted, unneeded, and unnecessary child, in order to survive in the outside world.

I knew that Harold had to go. I could not survive, homeless and in the real world, as the Harold who had no brains or talent and was an idiot, the Harold who took whatever abuse that came his way without as much as a whimper. I recognized that I had to find a new identity and put the old, introverted Harold far behind me so I could move on with my life as a stronger and better person.

For the first time in my life, I began making decisions on my own, and I was not being instructed on what to say and what to do by other people. No one was telling me what I liked or didn't like or to be seen and not heard. It was now time to decide who I was as a person and who I wanted to be going forward with my life.

I loved the challenge, but I was unsure of myself. I knew I had to abandon my lonely past, including my name; it just wasn't me anymore. I cherished being out in the world with other people, and I needed to quickly transition from a world where I was taught to be seen and not heard to a new world that seemed to be full of surprises and mysteries to explore. I had to learn how to interact with the new people I was meeting, people who actually appeared to like me and want to spend time with me. This was a brand new sensation.

I started with my name. I decided to change my name and start life over as someone stronger and smarter than Harold was ever allowed to be.

I didn't believe young Harold could have survived for one day out in the world all alone, let alone the months that I was homeless. Yet I knew that I was going to make it; I had to. This new person I was becoming was happy and positive and had no fear. I had become an explorer, and I had set out on a lifetime journey that I was excited to begin.

The transition that I needed to make wasn't going to be easy, but it had to be fast. I was, after all, homeless, and I was a stranger to my own neighborhood. Growing up, I hadn't been allowed out of the house, so no one other than the kids from school and my gang of friends from the street corner knew who I was or where I had come from. This turned out to be an advantage for me.

I vowed never to speak about my past or dwell on what could have been or should have been, just to move on and grow up. I was emotionally years behind other children my age, so I had to quickly develop myself morally, psychologically and intellectually. I needed to discover for myself who I was as a person and what kind of person I wanted to be going forward. What a great adventure this was going to be.

It amazes me how many childhood memories we carry with us throughout our lives without really thinking about them. Over the years I was often sent to my room without supper for some egregious thing I did. Back in those days, there were no televisions or computers in children's bedrooms to help them pass the solitary time. I did have my imagination, and books were my escape and salvation from the abuse.

My brothers had bookcases filed with books given to them over the years. I had none, but I would take one book at a time from their shelves and read it over and over. I would pass the hours in my room trying to stay out of everyone's way so that I would not commit some atrocity and be punished. All I wanted to do was immerse myself in the stories and fantasize about one day escaping the abuse and beatings. I wanted a life like my heroes and friends who were the characters in these books.

Anticipating my almost daily punishment, I stole my favorite two books from one of my brothers and hid them under the army cot where I slept. He'd been given the books as a Christmas gift, and he had never even opened the books much less read them, so he never realized that I took them. I loved getting lost in those stories, and I could recite whole chapters from them by heart all while conversing with my imaginary friends.

These two books were *The Adventures of Huckleberry Finn* and *The Adventures of Tom Sawyer*, both written by Mark Twain. Sometimes I couldn't wait to be sent to my room so I could escape into the world of Huck and Tom in peace and quiet. I dearly wish that I still had those original books to cherish, but they had to be left behind like everything else so that I could start over fresh.

Their pages were worn, wrinkled, torn, and dog-eared from use. Some of the pages were stained with tears, and a few from each book were tainted with a little blood from my constant bloody noses.

How could I not have related to these two young boys? Both Tom and Huck were lonely teenagers from broken homes who independently coped with the brutal world around them as best they could. Both were good kids but very mischievous, just like me. Both were runaways and great dreamers, believing that there was always something better just around the next bend in the river.

My favorite character of the two was Huckleberry Finn, and I closely related to him. He was the son of a drunk who lived his young life as a destitute vagabond. He was the typical innocent child who always seemed to find trouble yet always knew the right thing to do.

Looking back, I think I related to Huck more because his story was written in dialect. I could actually hear Huck telling his story as if he were speaking directly to me in his own words. He fascinated me, and we had many conversations with each other. He was my friend.

Over the years, I constantly dreamed about riding that raft down the Mississippi River with Huck and Jim, looking for freedom and adventure. I not only wanted to be with Huck, but I wanted to be like Huck. I wanted to live with him, to hang around with him, and to be his friend. I also was envious of the close friendship between Huckleberry Finn and Tom Sawyer, something I had never had.

Until my father entered the hospital and I first met my friend Jap, I had never experienced having a friend, let alone a relationship as close as those two boys enjoyed, and I craved that kind of friendship. I knew it had to exist somewhere.

In Mark Twain's autobiography, he wrote: "In Huckleberry Finn I have drawn Tom Blankenship, the true life inspiration for Huck, exactly as he was. He was ignorant, unwashed, insufficiently fed; but he had as good a heart as ever anybody had."

That is exactly how I decided I was going to live my life: not ignorant, unwashed and unfed, although at the time I was all three of those things, but with as good a heart as ever anybody had.

Because of the influence of these books, Huck was the first name that I thought I might take as my own to replace Harold. My only problem with it was that Huckleberry didn't seem like a name that would gather much respect in Trenton, New Jersey in 1970. Tom wasn't too bad, but I had a cousin named Tom, so that was out. Jim? Jim was the slave in the book, and I was running away from my own personal slavery and wanted no reminders of that, so Jim wasn't going to work either.

The impact those Mark Twain books had on me had been forever etched onto my conscience. I knew that somehow I had to take a name from these stories as my own, to carry forevermore. It was the only comfort I'd ever had in my childhood, and I not only wanted it, I needed it and had to have it.

I decided the name Mark, after Mark Twain, was too common. I needed something different to set me apart as an individual. I somehow knew that I wanted and needed to be a one of a kind.

Then it finally hit me: Hal. Hal Holbrook was a greatly respected actor who was predominantly known for his incredible portrayal of Mark Twain in a TV movie. He played him so well that everyone believed Hal Holbrook was Mark Twain. Taking the name Hal gave me an easy transition from Harold, and it also provided the close connection to Tom Sawyer and Huck Finn that I needed and that would stay with me for the rest of my life. Ironically, I learned many years later that Hal was a pseudonym and that Hal Holbrook's real name was Harold, something I never knew.

So I made the decision to call myself Hal. The young, introverted Harold was left with the arachnids and the dog crap in the dungeon of the English Manor, where I believe he still resides today. I moved on with my life to become a different, more independent, and stronger person.

Years later I was told by professionals that making this transition probably saved me a lot of therapy and potential mental problems. I was really just running away from it all. I was going on my own Mark Twain-type adventure down that river, in the raft, with my only two boyhood friends, Tom and Huck. Hal was born.

CHAPTER ELEVEN

LIFE OF PIE

The local hangout in the neighborhood was called the Roly Poly Restaurant. They had a pizza chief named Louie who must have seen something good in me, because he took a liking to me.

I would hang out for hours staring into the window of the pizza kitchen and watching Louie prepare the pies. Sometimes he would smile and wave to me, and I always gave him my biggest smile and waved back. I was mesmerized by the show he put on.

In the English Manor we never ordered take-out food—that wouldn't have fit in with the formal dinners—so we didn't know pizza. I wasn't even sure what this foodstuff was, but I knew it looked and smelled delicious.

After several days of seeing me gawk through the window, Louie came out on a cigarette break and sat on the stoop with me. He handed me my first ever slice of pizza and struck up a conversation while he smoked. I couldn't believe how good that warm little triangle-shaped slice of Heaven tasted. As many others in America can attest to, one taste of an East Coast pizza and you're hooked, addicted for life.

Louie spoke to me as a peer and seemed genuinely to care about me. We chatted during his smoke breaks every day for weeks, and when he asked me where I lived, I just replied, "In the neighborhood." But Louie had done his research and had found out that I was homeless.

Louie was the stereotypical Italian cook. He was short and chubby with a little mustache and looked very much like Chef Boyardee, only a little heavier. Looking back, I guess Louie probably felt sorry for me, and thank goodness he did.

Louie was a perfectionist and had developed a good pizza

business for the Roly Poly. One day he asked me if I was interested in learning how to make pizza. He advised me that if I learned that skill, I would always have a job somewhere, and I would never starve. I jumped at the chance, and he persuaded the owners to hire me even though I looked like a bum and actually was one. He promised them I would clean up and be presentable.

Louie stuck a chef's hat on my head and gave me a new, starched chef's shirt and pants to wear every day so that I would be clean and look fit to be seen in public.

It only took me a couple of days to learn the trade. Louie taught me never to touch the edge of the dough while stretching it out, because if my hands or even my fingers touched the edge of the pizza dough, it would flatten out and would not be perfectly rounded when baked. The dough would bake unevenly, leaving some of the crust soft and chewy and some of it well done or burned. A bite that was part crispy and part chewy at the same time was no good, according to Louie.

He taught me to knead and stretch the dough in circles slowly from the middle until it was one-third the size that the pizza should be when finished. Then he showed me how to pick up the dough gently while using my knuckles to stretch it a little at a time until it was the correct size to fit the pie pan. He said this technique gave the dough a nice, level texture and prevented it from becoming stretched too thin, which would cause holes to poke through and ruin the pie.

Last, Louie had to teach me the most difficult skill of making pizza. I had to learn to carefully slide the pizza dough off the wooden plank and into the oven, sometimes placing it in the back of the oven when other pizzas were already in the front. This was by no means an easy thing to do until I developed the special touch.

Our pizza oven held six pies at a time, so we often had to slide one over another inside the oven. That turned out to be the hardest part of making pizza. The dough board or paddle, called a peel, had to be floured perfectly. Too much flour and the pizza wouldn't cook right and the flour would eventually burn on both the oven and the bottom of the pizza. Too little flour and you couldn't fling the pizza off of the board and into the oven while still retaining its circular shape.

I created many a football-shaped pizza, and I had to cut out a strip down the middle and push the two ends together to get a circle so we could serve it to a customer, or I had to sell it by the slice.

I ruined quite a few balls of dough before getting the hang of it. Later I got the technique of picking up the dough, still without touching the edges, flipping it, and spinning it in the air. I would throw the dough high into the air for a more even stretch and a better-looking pizza, and also to put on a show for the customers in the window as Louie had done for me.

Some of the pizza parlors at that time would prepare the pies right in a kitchen window, much like the Roly Poly, putting on a spectacle by spinning the dough high in the air. Spinning didn't make the pizza bake any better or enhance the taste, but it did entice customers to come in and try a slice. Today, pizza dough tossing is a competitive sport, and a world championship is held every year complete with pizza dough juggling and acrobatics, proving that we might have been ahead of our time.

At the Roly Poly, I was earning money for the first time in my life. It was an amazing feeling to be self-sufficient. I ate well at the restaurant. As an employee, I got a free meal for every shift I worked, and I also got to eat my mistakes, those odd-shaped pizzas. It seemed that those mistakes coincidentally seemed to happen whenever I was hungry, or whenever my friends stopped by.

I was in pizza heaven. That job probably saved my life, or at the very least, it pushed me in the right direction, and I thank the owners of the Roly Poly forever. It also gave me a great work ethic. For the first time in my life I had money in my pocket, and after months of being homeless, I had some decent, fresh, hot food in my belly. I learned to understand the concept of being rewarded for hard work. I didn't think life could get any better than that. That is, until Louie, knowing I was a high school dropout, told me about a new school across town called the Chambersburg Street Academy.

I saved as much money as I could for the next few months and left my job at the Roly Poly with a good skill under my belt. I found a place to live on the other side of town in a place called Chambersburg, known simply as the 'Burg. This is where the academy was located.

I rented a third floor room in the 'Burg on Hamilton Avenue for $12.50 a week. There was a community bathroom one floor down. I didn't have a bathroom of my own, but a simple thing like taking a hot shower every day was incredible. I bought a one-burner hot plate and cooked my own food in the room. Dinner was usually a can of pork and beans or soup because I had to stretch the money I had saved to get me through school, but it was enough nourishment for me, and it seemed like a luxury.

The Chambersburg Street Academy was an experimental high school designed specifically for high school dropouts from the greater Trenton area. The school's mission was to get dropouts off of the streets and train them to pass a high school proficiency test so they could earn a General Equivalency Diploma (GED) and move on with their lives. There was no cost to the students, and the school was looking to fill classes for its inaugural year.

I marched straight in and enrolled at the Street Academy. A big guy named Johnny took my information and registered me. He looked at me and said, "Have you signed out of high school officially? Don't bullshit me kid!" I told him I had, even though I hadn't as I was determined to get my GED, and I needed the academy. I wasn't taking no for an answer.

I remembered this guy Johnny from Trenton High School. He was a few years older than me, and he'd been a senior there while I was a freshman. The reason I remembered him is that he was huge, the biggest kid I'd ever seen. Johnny was a good-looking guy, but people avoided him in the hallways if they didn't know him. The rumors were that he was the toughest guy in school and could kill someone with his bare hands.

As I got to know Johnny those few months at the academy, I never heard him say a bad word about anybody. I also realized that he was one of the nicest, most hard-working and honest guys I'd ever met. I'm proud to say we are still in touch and are friends to this day. The old adage is true that you really shouldn't judge a book by its cover.

I attended classes at the academy taught by people who were only a couple of years older than I was and were in their first jobs out of college, and I loved it. The classes were geared toward passing the GED test, so we were taught only subjects that would appear on the test.

Our classes were in two buildings on Anderson Street. The main building was a former movie house called the Park Theatre, which was directly across the street from The Casino. Despite the name, this wasn't a gambling casino (although you never knew what really went on in the back room or upstairs anywhere in the 'Burg). The Casino was a restaurant that had invented the famous Casino Dog which was their version of an Italian hot dog. The Casino Dog was a hot dog placed in a fresh, crusty torpedo roll made at a bakery just around the corner. Then the hot dog was layered with fried bell pepper and onions lightly cooked in olive oil, and topped with thick wedges of potato, which were fried quickly for a slightly crisp outer edge and a soft, steaming interior. Then the whole thing was lathered with spicy mustard. Yum!

Our time at the Chambersburg Street Academy was cut short as the school ran out of government funding and couldn't pay the teachers for more than a couple of months. Typical government bureaucracy to half-fund and then kill a greatly needed program. The faculty arranged for all of us students to take the GED exam before the academy closed for good.

A few days after the testing, the school's faculty got us all together and took well-deserved pride in announcing that the Chambersburg Street Academy was a resounding success. Every one of their students had passed the exam and had been awarded the GED on their first try—mission accomplished.

In addition, the staff had bragging rights as one of the academy's students had set a record for the highest GED score in New Jersey history. Surprisingly, I was that student. It must have been all that reading I did while hiding in my room.

It was then I first realized that maybe I wasn't an idiot, like my father had so often drilled into my head. Maybe I had a brain and some skills, just like everyone else. Maybe I could make it alone in the world. Maybe I wasn't really inferior to anyone but was actually an equal. This was my first real accomplishment in life and it felt amazing.

CHAPTER TWELVE

'BURG

The 'Burg was physically just the opposite of the western section of Trenton where I'd grown up and spent my homeless days. Chambersburg was created in 1872 and was spun off from neighboring Hamilton Township. It was first called the Borough of Chambersburg Township, and it was annexed to the city of Trenton in 1888. It is still known today by the name of Chambersburg, and unofficially its nickname is the 'Burg; I hope it always will be.

Chambersburg was magical to me. It was a wonderful Italian, family-oriented community where some of my high school friends lived. I fell madly in love with this part of Trenton. I remembered that my friends who lived there had always boasted about their loyalty to their close-knit families and friends from the 'Burg. They showed unconditional love for their parents and siblings, which was something new to me. Whole families were so close to each other they were inseparable. With them it was always, "blood, family first."

This section of Trenton was vibrant, and I was drawn to it like a moth to a flame. It was just a few square miles, and it was chock full of modest row homes. There was nothing extravagant about it, and certainly there were no mansions like there were in West Trenton. I marveled at the thought that these tiny row homes, equipped with only a couple of small bedrooms, could house so many happy family members with no one trying to kill each other.

The homes all had little front porches, and some were draped with simple awnings to block the sun and keep the house cool in the summer months. Most of the porches had lawn furniture consisting of no more than two chairs with a small, low table in between. A few had swinging wood or metal benches built for two that were hung from the ceilings with chains.

Each porch butted up to its neighbors' terraces on both sides, some separated by little flowerpots or larger flower boxes placed on the adjoining ledges to serve as a dividing line. Religious statues and figurines loomed everywhere. This neighborhood was so unlike West Trenton, which was dotted with large mansions deliberately built far from the neighbors, where very few people walked on the streets or even knew their neighbors by name.

In the evenings, the families would come out and sit on their porches right next to their neighbors and chat, sip some iced tea, wine, or a cup of espresso, and happily watch the world go by.

During the summers, many of these porches were filled with older Italian men playing scopa, an Italian card game, while small, thin cigars called stogies hung from their mouths as though they were surgically attached to their lips. The smaller dark, crooked cigars were soaked with anisette, and they smelled wonderful when lit.

Scopa cards weren't written in English but in various dialects of Italian—Piacentine, Napoletane, or Sicilian to name a few—so it was hard for me to learn the game. I loved to sit on the stoop and watch and listen to them play while they screamed and laughed in Italian to each other. These people were fascinating and joyful characters carrying on centuries of Italian tradition.

Chambersburg sported family owned and operated businesses on almost every corner. Bakeries, Italian restaurants, fresh fruit stands, cheese shops, and Italian delis. Shoe makers, jewelry stores, five and dimes, you name it; it was all within walking distance. The only time anyone had to leave the community was to go to work, and some didn't even have to do that.

Most people in the 'Burg worked in the factories of Trenton or were iron or steel workers. In the 1880s, John A. Roebling Sons Company built a large factory in Chambersburg to manufacture its wire rope. The wire rope was used on landmarks like the Brooklyn and Golden Gate bridges, and Roebling Steel employed thousands of people on 'round-the-clock shifts. Roebling Steel was so important to the 'Burg that there was an old, often-repeated joke: An Italian man who was immigrating through Ellis Island was once asked who the president of the United States of America was, and he replied, "John A. Roebling."

The 'Burg's streets were alive and bustling with wonderful, colorful characters going about their business in a family-friendly way. The 'Burg was almost identical to the Little Italy section of many major US cities.

Taking a walk down Hudson Street or Butler, Elmer or Mott Street, one could see, hear and smell the sights, sounds and aromas of old Italy. Children would play pickup ball in the middle of the street. Mothers would stroll down the sidewalks pushing baby carriages. People would stop each other on the street to say hello and chat for hours. The whole neighborhood was alive and vibrant.

It seemed that after school every schoolyard was packed with older kids playing ball and younger children on playground equipment with miniature rocket ships, swings and steel merry-go-rounds. That is, until someone hollered from their porch or rang a bell announcing that dinner was ready. Then the children would scatter like those river rats I'd run into not so long before. One resident offered what was my favorite dinner call every night. He stepped out onto his porch and blew his old army bugle to signal that it was dinnertime for his children. He loved that bugle and was so good at playing it that he was in demand to play "Taps" at the funerals of veterans, and he felt it was his duty to do so as long as his lungs would allow.

Each street was a virtual obstacle course of culinary delights. Neon signs hung from the second floors of many buildings proclaiming the Italian pleasures inside. Huge oak barrels and wooden crates sat in front of many stores, containing everything from fish to pickles.

Hot dried peppers hung from strings like Christmas decorations. Cheeses and meats dangled from ropes enticing passersby to stop and purchase. The local fruit vendor encouraged passersby to taste a piece of melon or an apple or a slice of cheese for free. Store windows were chock full of breads, pastries, tobacco products, and jewelry. Small, square tables on the sidewalks outside the many restaurants were adorned with red and white checkered tablecloths and umbrellas to protect the diners from the sun.

The people who lived in the 'Burg were hard workers who believed there was nothing more important than family. They believed families should live together and love together, forever. Sons and daughters grew up and bought houses next door to their parents. Cousins were always close by in the neighborhood. There was an unwritten law that every Sunday night was family dinner night, no excuses. Moms, dads, aunts, uncles, cousins, brothers, and sisters would pack into one of the 'Burg's small row houses for an Italian feast, which was actually a home-cooked culinary masterpiece the likes of which I'd never seen.

Those 'Burg mothers and grandmothers were no doubt the modern day Iron Chefs of America. They were passing down centuries-old recipes from the Old Country to daughter after daughter. The best chefs that I know today, both men and women, trace their culinary roots back to Chambersburg and are thankfully still using those recipes to keep the traditional food alive. I have a 'Burg friend from high school who is by far the best cook I've ever met, and we always joke that she should have her own television show in which she knocks on the door of any random home and bakes an incredible dinner from only what they have available at that moment.

And the wine, oh my! While the mothers were passing down those incredible recipes to their daughters, the fathers were passing down the formulas for homemade wine to their sons and grandsons. They taught their families the ins and outs of picking the right grapes, squeezing the juice at the right time, barreling, fermenting, bottling, and when it was ready, drinking. It all was based on centuries-old formulas that the men refused to let be forgotten by time.

The small basements in these row homes stored bottle after bottle of homemade wine. Some of the cellars had dirt floors, and they were always the perfect temperature for storing wine.

I was fortunate enough to be invited to many of these dinners by my new friends from the academy. Their normal Sunday meal would usually start with a little glass of the homemade wine, including a small taste even for the children. If the wine was store-bought, it was Chianti, either in a round bottle wrapped in a wicker basket or in a gallon jug that even the grandmothers would hook their thumbs into the handle and sling over their shoulders to pour.

Next, they brought out wonderful fruits and cheeses coupled with hot and sweet roasted peppers, olives, and a plate of fresh Jersey tomatoes sliced and topped with homemade mozzarella cheese, a pinch of basil and a drizzle of olive oil. Then some sort of fresh-caught fish cooked to perfection would appear from the kitchen. If I was lucky they would bring out a huge bowl of steaming fresh mussels cooked in an amazing white wine sauce.

Following the fish, the next course would be a huge bowl of homemade pasta and another giant platter filled with either pork, veal, sausage, or meatballs. Sometimes all four of the delicious slow-cooked meats made their way to the table. All were smothered with made-from-scratch gravy (actually tomato sauce, but known as gravy in the 'Burg) which had slowly bubbled and simmered on the stove all day long, tantalizing and teasing everyone's senses and causing many a stomach to gurgle. Next was the ritual of "fare la scarpetta". All this goodness had to be sopped up with a fresh loaf of Italian stick bread, not sliced with a knife but ripped off piece by piece as needed. Roughly translated from Italian the term "fare la scarpetta" means "do or to make the little shoe". The gravy left on the plates would be crying out for a little piece of bread to scoop up every last drop of the sauce leaving the plate almost clean enough to put right back in the cupboard.

I was blown away by the sight of families wanting and needing to be together—actually enjoying a meal together, laughing, teasing, and joking the entire time. It wasn't anything I had ever seen, and I had a hard time understanding what was going on. These dinnertimes were loud, boisterous events, celebrations. They were the opposite of our hushed formal dinners at the English family dinner table.

Our meals at the English Manor were military in fashion. We all sat around the table quiet as church mice, not daring to say a word. These Chambersburg families used dinner as a celebration of life.

Growing up, no music was allowed in our house, yet some of these folks played their radios or records and sang Italian songs right at the table during the meal. Almost everyone knew the words to songs by Sinatra or Dean Martin or Perry Como, whatever was playing, and they actually tried to out-sing each other. They embraced and enjoyed the simple things in life and each other. To me, it was an amazing concept.

After witnessing the wondrous lifestyle of Chambersburg, I knew this was where I had to be. I never wanted to leave, and although I wasn't Italian, I needed to belong to this neighborhood.

I saw a "Help Wanted" sign in the window of the Hudson Beer Garden on the corner of Hudson and Mott streets, which was right around the corner from my rooming house. It was a well-known, family-oriented, Italian bar and restaurant. I just strode into the Hudson, as it was affectionately called, with my biggest smile and all the nerve I could muster and told them that I was their new pizza guy. Louie was right. I would never want for a job with that skill.

The restaurant was one of the 'Burg's longtime legends. I remember listening to the local radio station and hearing the slogan, "I'm going to the Hudson," like it was yesterday. I finally felt like I belonged and had found a home.

One of the owners interviewed me. He was an ex-boxer in his 40s, and he ran the kitchen with an iron fist. Everyone knew he was the boss back there. He was about five-foot-six and of stocky build. Thick, jet-black hair was pushed straight back. He always had a heavy, rough beard. Even if he'd shaved in the morning, by nighttime he had thick, black stubble. He was quite the sight, never changing out of his white over-starched chef's shirt and pants. He even wore the uniform on days when he wasn't working. They were so starched that at night when he finally took them off to go to sleep, I think he must have stood them up in the corner of the room.

He lived in an apartment above the restaurant and always

talked about his dream of going back to the Old Country one day. Not just a chef, he also loved games of chance. He played poker in the neighborhood joints, but he loved craps better. He loved it so much that he often had guys over for a game in the basement of the restaurant. That way he could play all night, and if they needed him in the kitchen, he could just run upstairs and cook something. I don't think he ever left the neighborhood or made it back to Italy, but he was definitely the Don of Chambersburg to me.

At the time I applied for the job, I was cleaned up and was no longer looking like a bum, but I still had very long hair and wore it in a ponytail halfway down my back. When I walked in and asked for the job, he took one look at me and fell against a wall, holding his hand to his chest while laughing hysterically.

He asked how the heck a WASP (White Anglo-Saxon Protestant) hippy like me knew how to make tomato pies—another word for pizzas in Chambersburg. I laughed right back at him and said, "You just show me the kitchen and stand back and watch the magic." With that, we both went into the kitchen, and I made a couple of beautiful tomato pies for him. They were far better looking and more appetizing than the pies he made, because I never touched those rounded edges and the pies cooked perfectly. I even got cocky and flipped the second one high into the air, where it lightly scraped the ceiling, and it came down the perfect size for the pan. He was so impressed that he hired me on the spot.

Over time, we became great friends despite our age difference. Since both of us worked nights at the restaurant, we hung out together at the local fruit market across the street from the Hudson during the day while we weren't working.

The fruit stand was owned by a dapper older man and his wife. He was a short Italian gentleman who had thin white hair neatly combed straight back and a pencil-thin mustache that looked just like Errol Flynn's.

He was in great shape, and he was always dressed impeccably. Clearly overdressed for a fruit market vendor, he was considered both a ladies' man and a man's man. He was very soft spoken and always had a joke to tell. We spent many a lazy afternoon hanging out together at the market talking politics, women, and gambling.

Then there was the beauty salon a few doors down the street. The lady who owned it and I were instantly close. She was very beautiful and a hard-working mom. I quickly grew to love her dearly. She was one of the nicest and yet toughest women I've ever known, and some nights she would come into the Hudson and spend hours talking with me about anything and everything while I made the pies.

She had a daughter who was a couple years younger than me, and I thought she was one of the best-looking and also one of the sweetest girls in all of Trenton. Of course that meant she always had a boyfriend, which was too bad because I had a little crush on her. I know that her mom would have approved.

The ladies of the 'Burg would go to the beauty parlor to get their hair done and then come to the fruit stand to get their fruits and cheeses and a little flirting time with the ladies' man. His wife never seemed to mind, as she knew he was harmless. She would look at me and roll her eyes while he flirted. Of course, then I would begin shamelessly flirting with her, which made them both laugh.

I learned a lot about life in Chambersburg. I was grateful that the people took me in as one of their own. I learned a lot of 'Burg slang, like *stunad, mooshod, agida* and *maloik*. I can't believe how much I loved those characters, and sometimes I wish time had stood still and it could have gone on forever.

By hanging out with them I got to know many of the Chambersburg housewives. Most of them even wanted me to date their daughters, and they were always trying to set me up. I guess that since I was a hard-working guy, always with that big smile on my face, they felt that I would be good for their daughters. I became affectionately known around the community as "*Bionda Italiana*," the "blond Italian," and I was very flattered by the nickname.

Another memorable thing to me about the 'Burg was the churches. The church and religion played an important role in Chambersburg. People not only were proud of the 'Burg, but also of their parish. There were many places of worship there, but some of them stood out to me because of the large number of Sunday worshippers and because of their annual summer carnivals. The Immaculate Conception and Saint Joachim's Catholic churches each attracted 1,500 worshippers every Sunday.

Even though we were told we had signed up for church when I was thirteen years old, I'd yet to attend any religious services. It seemed as though everyone in the 'Burg went to church. Every Sunday morning the neighborhood came alive at the sounding of the church bells signaling for everyone to come out of their homes and attend the prayer services. Families dressed in their Sunday best outfits would answer the call of the bells and walk together down the street to church. It was both a religious and a social event.

Christmas Eve Mass was one of the biggest social events of the year. All the single teenagers just had to have a date for midnight mass and then breakfast after either home or more likely a local diner. Not having a date for midnight mass was like not having a date for the senior prom. You weren't with the "in" crowd and just not cool.

Each year since 1906, the entire neighborhood had gotten involved in the Feast of Lights. The feast was a religious ceremony celebrating Our Lady of Casandrino, or the Blessed Mother. This ceremony was complemented by a week-long carnival held in the middle of the street, highlighted by a Mass at Saint Joachim's and the Procession of the Madonna.

Most of us have seen a similar procession in the movie *The Godfather*, which was an amazingly accurate depiction. Six members of the Neapolitan Society would carry a statue of the Madonna from the church to a float, which then paraded through the streets of Chambersburg past all of the stores and row homes and crowds of spectators. The procession began on Butler Street and proceeded to Bayard, Mott, South Clinton, Elmer and Chestnut streets, passing hundreds of spectators and circling the neighborhood around the church. Several people carried a giant rosary in front of the float, which was followed closely by the women of the Fraternity of St. Clare praying the Rosary.

During the festival, Hudson Street was closed off in the evening to traffic and was lined with tents and concession stands. People came from miles around to taste the Italian culinary delights and try their hand at carnival games. Red, white and green flags displaying Italy's colors flew everywhere. From one end of the street to the other, you could eat hand dipped zeppoli, slices of tomato pie, sausage sandwiches with peppers and onions and gravy, calzones, stromboli, Italian ices and desserts, and pretty much anything Italian that you could imagine.

The Neapolitan Hall on the corner was set up as an old-fashioned beer garden and was always packed with patrons for dinner. Old time Italian music and Frank Sinatra, Dean Martin and Perry Como blared from outdoor speakers, and the place was abuzz with people. The locals called the Neapolitan Hall the "Nobbly Don." The Italian neighbors were rightfully proud of their neighborhood and their heritage and had every intention of passing it from generation to generation.

For the first time in my life, I witnessed true family love, both at the Hudson restaurant and in the community. The owners of the Hudson took me in as one of the family, and I worked very hard for them. I never missed a day and I was never late, and they responded by loving me back. One of the owners of the Hudson liked me enough to let me break a long-standing tradition at the restaurant. It seems they had a rule that the hired help could not date the owners' family members, ever. This man knew that his daughter, who was the hostess in the restaurant, liked me and wanted to ask me to take her to her high school senior prom. He gave me a heads-up and actually encouraged me to accept when she asked.

One thing he knew for sure was that I deeply respected him and would keep his daughter safe and take good care of her at her prom. After all, we were family. It was the first time someone had trusted me that way, and there was no way I would fail to earn that trust.

The matriarch of the Hudson family was Mama. Mama treated me better than my own mother ever had. She even communicated with me more than my own mother, and she didn't speak more than a few words of English. At the same time every night, Mama came to my end of the kitchen where the pizza ovens were and gestured with three fingers and her thumb curled up and placed to her lips, asking me, "Eat? Eat? *Mangia?*" Then she would gleefully make me a huge sandwich stuffed with sausage, meatball or steak and smothered with peppers and onions, or she would bring me a heaping plate of veal and peppers or lasagna, something different every day. Mama would then stand there with a big smile on her face to make sure I ate the whole thing. It made us both very happy to have her fatten me up a little, and she always got a "*Grazie tanto Mama*" (thank you very much Mama) in return from me.

Mama was the typical 'Burg grandma. She would affectionately call all the waitresses something in Italian and make them line up every night to see that their black and white uniforms were properly cleaned and pressed and that their shoes were as white as could be. Everyone loved Mama. She used to carry a salt shaker in her apron pocket and repeatedly sprinkle more salt on the Hudson's famous *pasta e fagioli* soup, whispering in broken English, "Shhh, they drink more."

I enjoyed working for the Hudson for the next couple of years. We experimented with sauce recipes and cheeses and changed the pizza dough formula. Together we built the pizza business from thirty tomato pie orders a night to more than a hundred pies a night.

All we did was put a little sugar in both the dough and the sauce to make it a little sweeter and crisper, and word went out. I shamelessly—but unsuccessfully—tried to mimic a world famous tomato pie restaurant a block away from the Hudson called DeLorenzo Tomato Pie. Like them, I started spreading the cheese over the dough first, and then I sprinkled the sauce on top of the cheese the way they prepared theirs. In no way did it look or taste anything like their tomato pies. Nothing tasted as great as their tomato pies, and the lines around the block of patrons patiently waiting to get a seat in DeLorenzo's tiny pizza parlor were a testament to that fact.

DeLo's, as the locals called it, sat near the corner of Hudson and Swan streets. It thrived there for more than sixty-five years. The founder opened the restaurant in the early 1900s, and he was another legendary Chambersburg character and a wonderful, gregarious person. He loved to regale his customers with stories. One of his favorite jokes was that he was such a lousy driver his wife had convinced him to give up driving their car before he hurt someone. So he bought himself a bicycle and ran over the mailman with it.

DeLo's tomato pies had a cult-like following. The restaurant was only open for business from 4 p.m. to 9 p.m., and it didn't even have a bathroom. People would wait in line outside and around the block all the way to the old Swan Street Ice House just to get their fix of this nationally award-winning food.

It was so good that their tomato pie was consistently named one of the top ten in the nation by various food magazines. The restaurant was even Zagat rated. They really knew how to make a pie. Its crust was extremely thin and well done, crispy. They put the cheese on the dough before the sauce. Their sauce wasn't even really a sauce at all. It was fresh plum tomato, crushed and spooned on top. Then, once the pie was baked, they would cut it at odd angles with a very small clam knife, producing a large crunch that would tickle your senses and make your mouth water.

Nothing said, "Dinner is ready" like the big crunch of a DeLo tomato pie being cut with that small knife. All this preparation was done in the middle of the tiny restaurant for everyone to watch and drool over while waiting for their turn to partake of the culinary delight. Tomato pie was the one and only thing on their menu.

Life was wonderful. I worked from five o'clock in the afternoon to one o'clock in the morning six nights a week, and after work I would hang out with the bartenders and help them clean up and close the Hudson's bar. We'd sit at the bar and have a couple of drinks, talking about anything and everything. I got to know all of the regular bar patrons and had a small following for my tomato pies. For the first time in my life I felt like a normal person who was respected, wanted, needed, and even loved.

I had made a close friend from the neighborhood whose name was Freddy. Freddy was a good-looking Italian kid with jet black hair combed straight back, and he wore a beard and mustache Van Dyke style that set him apart from everyone else. He was thin and handsome and very soft-spoken, especially with the ladies. He was a great kid who always had lots of cash in his pocket. His family owned another established family restaurant in Chambersburg, but Freddy didn't work there—he was a card dealer at a local joint run by some well-connected people. He loved that job, and he taught me to be a pretty good card player, too.

Because he worked nights dealing cards and I worked nights at the Hudson, we hung out together during the daytime. During lunchtimes we played together at all the local card joints, where we both won and lost a lot of money. The workers from Roebling Steel and other local companies would run over on their lunch hours to get a little card game in. Or, if it was a rainy day, the construction and iron workers would play because they couldn't work in inclement weather. Freddy taught me to play almost every card game, and to play them competitively. Poker, catch five, hearts, spades, ace duce, blackjack—you name it, we would partner up and play to win. We also played a lot of strip poker with the neighborhood girls, and somehow the girls always lost. Freddy could play a mean game of strip poker!

My first game of straight poker with strangers was my last. Freddy and I went to a joint called the Sugar Shack and played with some guys who were new in town. I was on a roll and had been drawing straights and flushes all day. For the last pot, only a freckle-faced kid known as The Swede and I were left playing. The pot was high, and I stayed in because I was on a hot streak and I'd been winning all day and also because his face had gotten bright red, so I thought he was bluffing. It turned out The Swede wasn't bluffing, and he had a low straight going into the draw. Before I took my last card, he bet everything he had, including the keys to an old Harley Davidson motorcycle.

I sat with the queen, jack, ten and nine of hearts. Open end straight flush going in. I could win by drawing any heart for the flush or any eight or king for a straight, and since I was up more money than I'd ever seen before, I called the bet with my cash winnings and drew the two of hearts. Not a straight flush, but enough of a draw to win myself a black and chrome Harley Davidson and a boatload of cash. Freddy and I decided that after that game, we would never play with strangers again; it was far too serious and dangerous.

I rode that bike all winter over the snow-covered streets of Chambersburg. Although I rode through the cold winter, it was tremendous fun trolling around on my Harley and being seen by all of the neighbors. I guess I was quite the sight. I had my long, dirty blond hair sticking out the back of the bike helmet, a leather waist-length jacket, tight Levi's jeans and knee-high suede lace-up boots. I made a lot of friends, but I didn't really care what anyone else thought about me, because I was free. I was independent and in my own world, with absolutely no one bothering me.

Freddy one day surprised me by telling me of a health problem he had. He'd been born with his intestine wrapped around his heart. As his body grew larger, the intestine squeezed his heart tighter and tighter, until one day the heart would stop beating.

He said there was nothing anyone could do to correct the anomaly, although these days it might have been rectified with open heart surgery. That surgery hadn't been invented yet, and at the time there was nothing the doctors could do. He knew his days were numbered, and Freddy lived a good, happy but too-short life in Chambersburg. He died in his sleep one night. I still remember him like it was yesterday, and I miss him dearly.

At Freddy's funeral, a few of his friends dedicated a Top Ten hit song called "Give Me Just A Little More Time," by a band called Chairman of the Board, as Freddy's song. We all swore that whenever that song came on the radio for the rest of our lives, we would stop whatever we were doing and talk about Freddy to whomever we were with. That way, he would live on forever within us. I don't know about the rest of the gang, but I still tell the story of Freddy whenever I hear that song. My children know of him, as well as anyone who happens to be near me when that song plays. Now, so do you. Rest in Peace, Freddy. May you keep drawing royal straight flushes and winning at strip poker for eternity.

CHAPTER THIRTEEN

BREAKING AND ENTERING

I was doing well—and much better than I'd expected—working at the Hudson Beer Garden and living in the 'Burg, but now my idyllic life was about to change drastically.

One summer night while I was cruising around the neighborhood on my motorcycle, I was pulled over by a cop named Dave. I knew Dave because he used to come into the Hudson with his patrol partner for a pizza. They always wanted a double-dough pie to go. I would put one piece of dough on top of another to make the tomato pie, which made it so thick that it barely fit into the box. I later learned this was similar to Chicago style deep-dish pizza. Dave and his patrol partner would get a six-pack of beer and my pie and go to Columbus Park to drink and eat their dinner. They claimed that the extra crust I made for them soaked up the beer so they didn't get drunk on duty.

When Dave pulled me over and asked for my license and registration, I had to confess that the motorcycle wasn't registered. Heck, I didn't have a bill of sale, a title for the Harley, or even a driver license. When I realized who it was who had stopped me, I pulled off my helmet so he could see me. Dave laughed and told me that he hadn't realized it was me, but that he had pulled me over because I had no license plate on the bike. He let me go with a warning, but he told me I owed him a double-dough pizza, which he came and ate the next day.

That's when it all started—that's when my view of the world through rose-colored glasses ended, never to be the same again.

My friends from the Hudson, much like Louie, were always advising me to get a college degree. They convinced me that it would be the only thing I ever have that no one could take away from me, so I decided to put myself through the local community college to get a business degree. Instead of continuing my education at the school of Hard Knocks I wanted to go to college. The problem was that if I went to school, I would have to travel outside of the safety of the 'Burg neighborhood with my illegal Harley, without a driver license, and without the security of my friend Officer Dave, who could easily be bribed with a pizza. I had no choice but to go legit and get my driver license. But this created another issue for me, because I didn't have a birth certificate; I had left home with nothing except the clothes I was wearing and I couldn't get my license without it.

As I was the black sheep of the family, I was not welcome in the English household, so I couldn't just walk up and knock on the door. I plotted to break into the English Manor and look for my birth certificate. I had heard from an old friend from West Trenton that my mother and siblings were out of town staying at the Jersey Shore for a few weeks that summer and that the house was empty. They were at a house in Beach Haven that my father had purchased shortly before he died.

While my father was alive, he'd had an office in the original formal dining room of the mansion, where he treated private patients on Saturdays. His office was off-limits to the children so I had never seen the inside of it, but I knew it would be the best place to search for my birth certificate.

I knew where the spare key to the house was kept, and since no one was at home, breaking in was as easy as picking up the key and walking into the house. I went straight into the office and started looking around.

As a first-time visitor to a psychiatrist's office, I didn't know what to expect. The office was furnished with a huge carved wooden desk with an oversized swivel chair upholstered in black leather with brass rivets around the edges. Next to the desk was a matching leather chair that didn't swivel. Directly across from the desk was the classic psychiatrist's couch, also in matching black leather with brass rivets.

A rolling stainless steel cart stood next to the couch, with both a blood pressure kit and a syringe needle sterilizer on it. Sitting on another table near the window stood a strange-looking machine that I couldn't figure out. That turned out to be my father's electroshock treatment equipment. My father would hook patients to it with wrist straps and small clamps, like battery jumper cables, and ask them questions. If he didn't like the answers, he gave them a jolt of electricity until he got the responses he wanted.

The office also contained a modified reel-to-reel tape recorder. My father would experiment with a treatment called "psychic driving." He would put a set of headphones over his patients' ears and a padded blindfold over their eyes and turn on the recorder. The patients would listen to the same customized message repeating itself again and again. "You will not touch a cigarette again," for example—different messages for different patients and different problems.

One patient I distinctly remember was Charlie. His only problem seemed to be that he stuttered. Charlie would come to the office every Saturday, and I could see him from the front yard through the window with those headphones on. "You will not stutter. You will not stutter."

Then there was Mary, whom I met later in life. Mary's parents sent her to my father every Saturday for what she later told me was at least a year of therapy. She was sixteen years old, and her parents thought she was too boy crazy, so they felt she must need psychiatric help. My father put the headphones on her for an hour at a time to listen to the message, "I don't like boys. Boys are mean." "I don't like boys. Boys are mean." I'm surprised she still liked boys after that, although she's been divorced three times, so either the therapy worked or it may have caused her lasting issues.

One wall of the office was covered by a cabinet with locked glass doors, where my father kept his supply of drugs. As a psychiatrist, he was a medical doctor and could legally prescribe medication, and he kept a stock of various drugs on hand to test on his patients. Another wall in the office held a large row of file cabinets, where my father kept his patients' records. I was sure my birth certificate would be in those files.

As I didn't want to alert the neighbors that I was in the house and have them call the police, or worse yet, my mother, I'd brought a small flashlight with me so I wouldn't have to turn on any lights. I put the flashlight in my mouth and pulled open a file drawer that was marked "A, B, C." I started flipping through the hanging files in the drawer, looking for the letter B for birth certificate. Suddenly and surprisingly I came across a file in the front of the cabinet simply labeled "Adoption".

I don't know why, other than curiosity and the fact that I always seemed to have the uncontrollable urge to do what I wasn't supposed to do, but I pulled out the file and opened it. In the file was an old, yellowed, tri-folded document titled, "In the Matter of Adoption of Children by Harrison F. English, Certified Copy of Judgment of Adoption."

I couldn't believe what I had in my hands. I held the document closer to the flashlight and looked it over. I had brief thoughts of putting it back, as I knew no one had ever wanted me to see it, and I also wasn't so sure I wanted to know what or who it was all about.

Put it back? I couldn't have put it back if I'd wanted to. My hand was frozen, the paper stuck to it like it had been glued there. Pandora's Box had just been opened, no going back now.

My mind was racing, and I could hear and feel my heart rapidly pumping the blood through my veins. I opened the document from the Mercer County Surrogate's Office and I now had Case No. 4340 in my hands.

I read that someone by the name of Vernon Lee Handley had given his permission for his three children to be adopted by Harrison Force English. The three children's names were listed in the document, and one of them was Harold Earl Handley. It felt like I'd been hit in the chest with a hail of searing-hot bullets.

I was so shocked that my mouth gaped open and I dropped the flashlight, smashing it into several pieces on the hardwood floor. It was now pitch black, so I had no choice but to fumble my way to the door and turn on the overhead light in the office, even though my action might alert the neighbors that there was an intruder in the house.

As I examined the papers more closely, I read these words in the document "the best interests of the children would be promoted by such adoptions." I thought that was the most outlandish statement that I had ever heard.

I began having a series of flashbacks to events in my life, all having to do with Harrison Force English. I remembered things that had happened over the years that were confusing to me at the time but now seemed significant and finally crystal clear. I stood there, wobbly, while images of Harrison's actions over the years flashed before my eyes. These visions and the dizziness made me sick to my stomach, and I staggered to the couch so I wouldn't faint or regurgitate.

Time and space seemed to stand still. I became short of breath and had to put my head between my legs so that I wouldn't pass out. My face was burning and my head felt like it was blowing up like a balloon that might burst at any minute. Everything was in slow motion, and it felt as though I were in a compression chamber or a pressure cooker. I sat there for what seemed like a long, long time while holding my head in my hands to stop the swirling merry-go-round of emotions.

Now the revelations started. First, I had an image of that judge in his chambers on my thirteenth birthday a few years earlier. Immediately I realized what that day had been all about. We weren't signing up for church—it was an adoption. That's what the judge had meant when he'd asked me those thirteen unlucky and fateful words: "Do you understand what we are doing here today and do you agree?"

I was duped and had unwittingly agreed to be given up for adoption. I now couldn't help but wonder what would have happened to me if I had said no on that day, no I don't understand, and no I don't agree. Would I have been immediately shipped off to my biological father? Or would I have been sent to St. Michael's Orphanage or admitted into the Trenton Madhouse? I wondered about the reasons for the secrets, lies, and deceit. Why not just tell us the truth, what could be the harm in that, who would even care?

My mind was playing games and flashed further back to when I was ten years old and I had first asked my father if I could join the Little League baseball program with some of my school friends. He wouldn't allow me to play baseball and had scolded me, saying the reason he wouldn't let me was that I had never shown any interest before and that I would probably be lousy at it anyway. Never mind the hours I'd spent each day throwing a tennis ball against the house, pretending that I was on a baseball team and shagging fly balls.

The real reason he wouldn't let me play was because I would have needed a birth certificate to join a baseball team. My birth certificate before I was thirteen years old must have had my natural father's name on it, not Harrison's. The first of our many family dark secrets would have been revealed.

Then I remembered an event that had occurred when I was eleven years old and sharing a bedroom with my two younger brothers. I was pretending to be asleep in the little army surplus cot that I slept on every night. My brothers each had a much more comfortable double bed, but I'd never thought about that until now.

Harrison came into the bedroom to tuck us all in, and he didn't even look at me lying in my cot pretending to be asleep. He first walked over to one brother, tucked the covers in around him, and leaned down to kiss him goodnight. Then he tiptoed to my other brother's bed and tucked him in, leaned down, and kissed him goodnight. I was expecting him to visit me next, and I hoped he wouldn't know that I was pretending to be asleep. But he just turned around and walked out of the room without even looking at me, let alone tucking me in. What about me? I'd wanted to shout, "Hey, you forgot about me!" but I was afraid I'd be punished.

Then I had a flashback to when I was fourteen years old. My younger brother and I were fighting like brothers normally do, when he picked up a hammer and started swinging it at me, shouting, "Who's the handsomest son?" I playfully chased him around a corner of the room, and he banged into the wall hard enough and in such an angle as to break his collarbone.

Harrison came rushing out of his office like a madman. He picked up a pool cue from the billiard table in the adjoining game room and began hitting me while my brother lay on the floor writhing in pain.

He hit me with the pool cue square on the top of my head, causing the stick to break in half. Then he threw the stub at me and picked up another one. He kept swinging the stick, repeating, "Don't you ever touch my son again or I'll kill you!" His next swing injured my finger as I used my hand to shield my head. I had to set and bandage the sprain on that finger myself because he wouldn't even look at me. I used two pencils and Scotch tape to set the finger and left it like that for a week. I remembered at the time thinking what did he mean, "Don't you ever touch my son again?" Why did he say that, but I chalked it up to his being mad and upset at what happened.

Another time, when I was about thirteen, I drew myself a hot bath on a Sunday night. Just as I was preparing to get into the tub, in came Harrison, screaming at me that I had taken all of the hot water and he couldn't give his son a bath now, all the while smacking me in the face hard enough to knock me into the tub and once again breaking my glasses on the tile floor. I remember that I went to bed and lay there soaking wet in my clothes all night, and that tub of water sat unused until someone else emptied it the next day. That was the last bath I dared to take in the English Manor. But I never could comprehend what he really meant by "give his son a bath".

The last memory was of a few years back when my younger brother, who was born with only one kidney, had a problem with the one that he had. When I heard from my mother that a person only needed one kidney to survive, I volunteered to donate one of mine to him. My father scoffed at me. He just laughed and told me that mine would not be good enough. At the time, I didn't realize how right he was; I just took it as though there was something wrong with me. Now I knew the real reason was that it wouldn't have been a DNA match for my brother, and that would have required some serious explaining.

So many memories of events long past were exploding like fireworks in my conscious that I shook my head to try to make them stop.

After what seemed like hours, I got the strength to stand up and proceed with my mission. I opened the other file in the cabinet and found what I'd originally been looking for—my birth certificate. *This isn't over yet,* I thought as I left the office with both documents stuffed under my motorcycle helmet. *In fact, it's only just begun.*

Later I discovered that the reason for the secret adoption on my thirteenth birthday was that my older brother had just turned seventeen years old and went to the Motor Vehicle Department to get his driver license. He brought with him the required copy of his original birth certificate. The license was then issued to him with his real birth name on it, Handley. It wouldn't do to have any evidence of that lying around to be seen. Someone might have gotten wise or asked questions.

Because of the adoption, my mother and my father—now forever known to me as my stepfather—thought their dirty little secret was safe. After the adoption, they could actually produce birth certificates for us. These certificates had the last name English written on them and Harrison actually listed as our birth father. Our original birth certificates with a different name, Handley, were now sealed away by court order forever, never again to see the light of day.

I can't begin to describe what a feeling of wholeness it would give me to hold my original birth certificate in my hand one day and not the one listing Harrison as my natural father, but legally that cannot happen.

Mark Twain once said, "The two most important days in your life are the day you are born and the day you find out why." Well, to me, this was the day I was born; now the mission was to find out why.

Why was all this kept a secret? Who cared, and what could possibly have been such a big deal?

I knew I had to find my biological father some way, somehow, someday. I really had no means of finding this person named Vernon Lee Handley, but I resolved that I would die trying.

Later that night, my mother found out that I was at the house because a neighbor saw me through the window when I'd dropped the flashlight causing me to turn on the overhead light. Some thief I was. The neighbor called her at her Beach Haven shore house to tell her I was there, in the house. My mother panicked and cut short their vacation. She packed up and rushed home with the younger children that very night.

I now know that she was afraid of something that she'd thought I might have found in the office, but I didn't realize it then. As soon as she got home, according to my sister, she lit a bonfire in the psychiatric office's garbage can. She poured in lighter fluid and lit papers on fire. She went on a destructive, furious rampage, opening drawers and cabinets and burning every file in the office and in the house while the younger siblings looked on in confusion.

My sister, who was only thirteen years old at the time, witnessed the destruction. She told me in later years that our mother burned pictures, documents, and folders. A large stack of letters written in German with red and blue stripes on the envelopes—indicating airmail—hit the flames. It turned out that what she burned was everything even remotely connected to her family's past, our family's past. She left no evidence of our youth, her childhood, or her German heritage after that night.

I learned that she burned pictures and documents relating to her own childhood and family in Germany. My sister said there were pictures of my mother's two brothers in military uniform that went up in flames. She thought that the brothers, our uncles, might have been wearing Nazi SS uniforms. That might have explained the fire. Perhaps she was trying to conceal things that her family may have done in Germany during the war.

Official-looking documents written in German were eradicated. It seemed that she tried to burn my entire childhood and anything connected to it. I'll never understand why my mother would destroy mementos and things that any normal mother would want to cherish and keep for her children forever.

I only wish she could have incinerated my horrible memories of her husband, Harrison, and the years of beatings and mental abuse. Those recollections are scorched in my charred memory forever.

As I was writing this book, my sister gave me a precious gift that I wish I had seen and taken with me that night many years ago when I broke into the office. The gift she gave me was my baby book. It was titled: *Baby's Own* ___. I don't know what the last word of the title was, because it was thrown into that bonfire and the flames burned a portion of the cover. It is a hardback baby diary outlining my family tree. It names my real father, my mother, my grandparents, and others. My sister somehow felt the need to rescue it from the trashcan after the fire simmered down. She had no idea what it was or why she wanted to save it, but she felt she had to hide it from my mother so that it could survive and someday be given to its rightful owner, me.

Even at the young age of thirteen, she knew what was happening just didn't seem right. The book is the only item of evidence that survived the bonfire that night. It was only partially burned, as its hard cover was laminated and wouldn't catch fire. In those days, it was common practice for publishing companies to laminate baby journals so that they would last the entire lifetime of the child. How ironic?

I cherish that book because it is all I have of my childhood. I still don't understand how any parent—mother or father—could set ablaze their child's heredity and history like that. But then again, I still can't comprehend this whole scenario as it unfolds.

As soon as the wastebasket flames subsided that same night, my mother called in the reinforcements. She placed a call to Robert, a friend of hers who was a steelworker standing six feet four inches tall and weighing more than three hundred pounds. He'd been a part-time handyman around the English Manor for years and was a pretty intimidating guy.

At about three o'clock in the morning, Mom and Robert came banging on my rooming house door. I have no idea how they knew where I was living, but somehow for some reason she'd been keeping tabs on me. They came to threaten me and to demand that I give back anything that I took from the office. They woke my neighbor on the first floor of the rooming house and he had to come upstairs to wake me, but thankfully he hadn't let them in.

I went downstairs, and Robert demanded everything I "stole" from the house or he was going to beat the hell out of me and call the cops to lock me up. My mother stood behind him with an empty stare on her face and never uttered a word during the entire confrontation.

I was still on an adrenaline high from discovering my true identity earlier that night, and I felt empowered. I was eighteen years old now and a legal adult, and this apartment was my home. I knew they had no right to be there, and I wasn't going to let them scare or intimidate me. I also knew that if they called the police that it would be my friend Dave who would answer the call, and no way was I going to jail—that would be the end of Dave's free double-dough pizzas.

I stood tall and looked them both straight in the eye and told them I hadn't stolen anything, but I admitted that I took my birth certificate, which legally belonged to me and not to them. I never mentioned the adoption papers, which were spread out on my bed upstairs. I told them that if they didn't leave immediately, I would be the one to call the cops. Then I slammed the door in their faces, telling them that I never wanted to see either of them again. That was the last time I saw my mother for several years.

After they left, I realized that there must have been much more information in the office that my mother wanted kept secret, or they never would have paid me that three a.m. visit. I also realized she had no clue what I took that night, and the strange look on her face was born of fear for what else I might have discovered. I then believed that I must have messed up and overlooked something else, something even far more important or even dangerous.

It was that Huck Finn attitude of always wanting to do the right thing that made me leave Harrison's office with only those two items that night. I knew both were rightfully mine, and no one could take them away from me. For years after that night, I wished I hadn't had that always do-the-right-thing drive. What else I could have discovered that night if I had stayed and ransacked the office may have been even more life-changing. I doubt that I would have understood most of it, but I would have at least seen the documents and pictures before they were burned to ashes. Had I found that baby book, I would have immediately found my natural father.

I never could have imagined the rest of the secrets of the English family that were yet to be exposed.

CHAPTER FOURTEEN

FACTORY AND THE UNION

Several years after the night I found out about my adoption, I got married and was offered a great-paying job working for the General Motors Fisher Body Division. I proudly worked on the assembly line there for ten years with wonderful people.

The Inland Fisher Guide Plant was a General Motors facility located in Ewing Township. It opened in 1938 as one of GM's most modern plants, and it was a vibrant factory for sixty years. The factory was initially part of the Ternstedt Division of GM's Fisher Body unit and was used to manufacture auto parts.

The plant manufactured body side moldings, chrome door handles, and many other interior components. During World War II, the facility was converted to build thousands of torpedo bombers called Avengers for the United States Navy as part of GM's Eastern Aircraft Division. Future President George H. W. Bush was shot down by Japanese anti-aircraft fire while piloting one of the Avengers that was built in Ewing. After that incident, the story goes, navy pilots would look inside the nose of the Avengers to see if they were made in Ewing, because those were the airplanes they wanted. Since George Bush had survived the crash, they wanted the solid, well-built planes that were made in Ewing Township.

With a population of almost four thousand workers in the plant, seniority ruled the day. Whoever worked at the plant the longest had first choice of shifts and jobs in the factory, and the date of hire meant everything. Those workers who were hired more recently had low seniority and had to work whatever hours and jobs were left over.

I had little seniority, so I was always getting bumped around on three different shifts—days, nights and midnights—and into different departments in the plant. It was many rough years, but it turned out to be a really good thing for me.

I'll never forget my first couple of days in the factory. I was walking up the steps to the cafeteria for lunch one day when a little old lady who looked like my grandmother pinched my rear end and said, "Yum, fresh meat to mess with." I was in shock not because of what she did or said, but because I had never seen an older person do anything like that before. She could have been my grandmother, after all. I was in culture shock, and I needed to learn fast how to survive in the factory world.

It was hard work, and that was my first lesson in tough women and the many different ways those women survived their years of factory life. Women played an especially prominent role during wartime. The men were away from home serving overseas and the women were working the factories and raising their children alone.

I ran into my friend Irish Murf from the old neighborhood; he also had a job there, and he and I worked the assembly lines for years.

It broke my heart when General Motors closed that plant and the workers lost their jobs. Today I can't drive down Parkway Avenue past the site of the old factory without tears in my eyes. Hundreds of us were in our twenties and were hired into the factory at the same time when they added a third shift to production. We grew up together in the factory.

A small number of people working at General Motors were not so nice; I had run-ins with some of them later. The vast majority were salt-of-the-earth type folks, many of whom are my friends to this day.

The United Auto Workers (UAW) union represented non-management employees. It was a great international union, but a union is only as good as its local leadership. It seemed to some of us rookies that a few, but not all, of the local union leaders were all about taking care of themselves and their friends.

The president of the union was of retirement age and didn't believe in changes even if they were desperately needed. He believed in status quo, and his favorite saying was, "It's always been that way, so why change it now?" The shop chairman, who turned out to be the real boss of the local union, was a tough man who knew politics like nobody's business.

Not many of us young rookies cared much about the union. We were busy raising our young families and trying to survive in this new world. However, when we needed the union for any reason, we expected to be well represented, and we resented it if we weren't. After all, we had to pay big union dues each payday for the privilege of working in the factory.

It seemed to me that ninety percent of a union officer's time was spent on ten percent of the workers. We actually called them the "ten percenters." They were people who used the system for their own advantage, didn't give a fair day's work for a fair day's pay, and generally abused the system. They were frequently late or didn't show up to work on the assembly lines, which meant all of us had to work harder until they showed up. Then, when they were reprimanded—or "written up," as management called it—a few of the union reps would fight like crazy for them, trading off a good worker's legitimate grievance to get their friends off the hook.

We used to gripe to each other about these conditions, but we never did anything about them until one day when I just couldn't take it anymore. A foreman supervising our assembly line was known for abusing workers, especially women. A friend of mine was assigned to pack the seat adjusters at the end of the assembly line. Seat adjusters are the manual assembly unit under a car seat that a driver uses to move the seat forward and backward.

My friend was eight months pregnant with her first child, and the seat adjusters weighed about ten pounds each. She had to lean over a steel basket and pack thousands of them coming off a moving assembly line during the eight-hour shift. It was summer and about one hundred ten degrees in the plant. About an hour into the shift, I called the union representative and the foreman over and asked if I could switch jobs with her. I had an easier job that allowed me to sit down, and it would have been better for her.

The foreman looked at the union rep and then at me and said, "That's how I like my women, pregnant and bent over, and I'm enjoying watching her." I couldn't believe he said it, and I told the union rep that I wanted to file a grievance against the foreman for that statement. Well the two were fishing buddies, and the union rep refused to do anything about it. When I started yelling at him and told him he was useless, he said, "There's an election coming up and if you don't like it, why don't you just run for office and do something about it, you troublemaking idiot?" They both walked away laughing at me.

Idiot? Did he just call me an idiot? Not the word I wanted to hear. I didn't need to be reminded of Harrison, as I'd now come to call my stepfather, nor of the lunatic asylum.

A couple of months later there was a plant wide union election, and I did do something about it. The president of the union was retiring, and my friend Irish Murf and I raised some money and put together a team of candidates for the various union positions. Murf insisted I run for president and most of us were victorious, and I was surprised to be elected president. Afterward, that union rep wasn't very happy being put back to work on the assembly line after so many years as a rep. Word got out that the party was over, and the older union reps, even the good ones, began retiring in droves, allowing the youth to take over.

It was a great job being president of the union. I grew up fast and was the boss for the first time in my life. All of the newly elected officers worked hard and changed everything that we thought was wrong with the local union. In addition to the usual union summer picnic exclusively for members, we included a family day at Great Adventure Amusement Park with a private picnic catered all day, free parking, and tickets to the amusement park. Workers met each other's spouses and children for the first time in the fifty years of the plant's existence.

We rejuvenated the various union committees, updated technology at the union offices, and literally cleaned up the union hall and its bar. No more worker grievances were traded off for friends, and General Motors got rid of some of the bad apples, the "ten percenters," which was a good thing for everyone. We instituted joint labor/management training programs, and instead of treating workers like robots with no minds of their own, management began to value the minds and experience of the talented workforce as assets.

The new policies negotiated by the shop committee kept the plant open and in operation for an additional eight years after General Motors first announced it would be closed. Those precious eight years allowed more workers to become eligible for retirement, in better position to put their children through college, or just pay down their mortgages with the advanced notice of closing. Many workers went on to different GM plants all over the country in order to accumulate their thirty years and be able to retire at full pension and health benefits negotiated by the union. To those workers who stayed and ground out a tough living I give my utmost respect.

The most rewarding experience I had was negotiating the contracts that affected people's lives. We were an amalgamated local union, which meant I represented workers in several facilities in the Trenton area in addition to the GM plant. One such place was a local steel plant. It was a custom steel company, a small shop in Trenton with about twenty employees and a long history of bad blood with management. The workers went on strike and picketed the place once each year at contract renewal time. This strike became a tradition and went on year after year, sometimes lasting for months.

Shortly after assuming office, I got a call from the company management informing me that they we closing the factory and selling to another company. I asked them when this sale was taking place, and they said, "Right now, this afternoon." I couldn't believe I'd had this hot potato thrown at me in my first few weeks in office.

Our newly elected recording secretary was in the union hall when I got the call, and I asked him if he wanted to take a ride with me to put out a fire. He and I drove over and met a man named Al who was waiting for us in the lobby.

Al was an old-time steel guy who had already spent a very successful lifetime in the steel business, and he was the new proposed buyer of the plant. We spent about an hour getting to know each other, and it was clear to me that he was a good and honest man who put all his cards on the table. Al explained the deal plainly and simply. He needed the workers to hold an election on the spot to see if they approved of the sale of the company to him, and if they would honor the existing contract for another year with no changes and no strike. He pledged that if they did, he would take care of them in future years.

From my telephone conversation with the company executives earlier, I knew that either this sale went through successfully or the plant would close, putting twenty workers and union members permanently out of a job.

Our recording secretary and I went onto the shop floor and called the workers into the middle of the plant so I could address them. Me—a newly elected and wet-behind-the-ears union leader. My remarks were short and sweet. I told them what was going on and that if they voted to support the sale to Al, they would continue to work under their existing contact and, most importantly, they would keep their jobs. I told them I believed in Al and that I thought working conditions under his ownership would improve. I said I was confident that there would be no more yearly strikes. Finally, I told them that if they voted no, the plant would close immediately and everyone would be out of a job. It seemed like a no-brainer vote to me.

Well, our recording secretary called for a vote by a show of hands, and it was a tie. Ten workers were for the sale, and ten workers were against the sale. I had to think quickly, so I turned to the workers and proclaimed that the president of the union was authorized to cast a vote in the case of a tie, and that I was casting a vote to approve the sale. I still have no idea if that was allowable under the UAW constitution, but I felt I had to do something to protect these workers; I had to protect ten of them from themselves.

Twenty years later that steel plant is still operating. Al's son is now running the place. Once in a while I bump into one of the workers from that historic day at the plant. They tell me stories about how much Al treated them with respect and improved their workplace and their lives, and how grateful they were to me for doing what I did. They brag about their wonderful retirement pensions. I get the same kind of response from those who voted no to the sale that day on the shop floor. It's very rewarding.

CHAPTER FIFTEEN

THE SEARCH

As president of the union, I was asked to serve on the national bargaining committee. I got to travel to almost every major city in the country. I was routinely traveling one week each month, and this afforded me the opportunity to conduct a search for my real father. The Internet hadn't been invented yet, so I had to go about the search differently than one would today.

In each city I visited, I would pick up a local phone book and look for the name Handley. If I found any Handley in the book, I would write a note asking if they were related to Vernon Lee Handley or knew of him. I sent notes for three years and only got one answer. It was from a widow from Indianapolis, Indiana. She wrote me back and told me that she still used her husband's name in the phone book for security reasons but knew little of his family, and so she couldn't help me. She said she would pass the letter on to the Handley side of her family.

Being president of the union also meant being involved in local politics. I had the good fortune of meeting a newly elected congressman from my district who was a decent, honest politician. (Isn't that an oxymoron?) I believed in this honorable man, and we quickly became friends. It is no surprise to me that he is still serving in Congress today. Our wives became friends as well, and he offered my wife a job as the scheduler in his congressional district office. What an honor for my wife to work for a United States Congressman.

Every year the congressman would host a Christmas party for his staff, both from Washington and from his New Jersey district. One year I had a few too many glasses of wine at the party and got into a deep conversation with a member of the staff. She was the manager of the congressman's southern New Jersey office, and after what she did for me that year, she's now family.

Somehow our conversation turned to family and my search for my natural father. She was the first person outside of my immediate family in whom I'd ever confided what little information I had about being adopted.

The Christmas season had always been the most disheartening time of the year for me. Each year I got a little depressed about not knowing who my father was and not being able to find him.

Monday morning came, and I got a telephone call from her. She said things were slow in the office and she couldn't stop thinking about my story. She asked me if I could tell her any more details beyond what I had shared at the party.

I told her that my father might have been in the military. My oldest brother was born in Waiblinger, Germany, in a town that was a suburb of Stuttgart. My other brother was born in Ft. Knox, Kentucky, and I was born a year and a half later, also in Ft. Knox. The towns where we three boys were born each had a United States Army base nearby. I surmised that there was a chance my father was a military man. Also, if he spent more than four years in the army, he might have been a "lifer," serving twenty years or more.

She responded that through her work in the congressman's office, she knew a person in Washington, DC, who mailed out the US Army pension checks each month. She said she would call her contact and see if he could help point us in the right direction.

Not fifteen minutes later she called me back, trying poorly to hide her excitement. She said, "Listen, this may or may not be anything, so please don't get your hopes up." She continued, "My contact actually personally knows a Vernon Lee Handley and also served in Vietnam with him." She said her contact would be willing to get in touch with him for us.

Her contact said I should write a letter to Mr. Handley and seal it in an envelope with my name on the outside. He said he would send it along with the next pension check with a note of explanation. In his note to Vernon Lee Handley, he would explain that he didn't know the enclosed letter's sender nor did the sender know Mr. Handley's address. The note would say that no personal information had been disclosed. He told her he would do this even though he would be risking his job, because the Vernon Lee Handley that he knew and had served with was a friend and a good man.

I wrote that letter immediately, although it took about two dozen versions to get right. The staffer asked if I would allow her to read it before I sealed it in the envelope. She said that when she read it, she cried.

Off went the letter. I had the feeling this could turn out to be another dead end. But on the other hand, maybe not, and it was certainly worth the shot. I wrote:

Dear Mr. Handley,

My name is Harold Handley English and I am writing this letter with high hopes that my years of search for my natural father are close to an end. I hope that my letter does not offend you, and I sincerely hope that you will recognize my sincerity in wanting and needing to know what's been kept from me all of these years. This is, by far, the hardest letter I have ever written as there is so much I want to say and can't seem to find the right words.

My search began in 1970 when I first learned that I and my two older brothers were adopted by Harrison English. For some reason, which I cannot comprehend, he and my mother felt it necessary to hide that fact from us.

Since that time I have not been quite the same, knowing that I have a natural father I don't remember, but at the same time love very much.

I have a wife and a five-year-old daughter, and family is the most important thing in my life. Each year at Thanksgiving and Christmas time I seem to dwell on thoughts of my father. He turns up in conversations with my closest friends. All of whom have been most supportive and have kept me going through the many false leads I have been following these years.

I don't want to impose or disrupt anyone's life. That is the last thing I would do. If my search is indeed ended, it would mean so much more than anything in the world to me and I would be grateful for any return word. I am not looking to walk into my father's life at this stage and disrupt it. But I feel I have to take the chance to at least communicate by letter.

I was going to enclose a picture of myself and wife Diane and daughter Rachael, but I don't want to move too fast, and this may indeed be another dead end in my search.

I don't know if it's fate or irony that I received the chance to send this letter during National Adoption Week and during the Thanksgiving and Christmas season, but whichever it is I am more than willing to take the chance.

Below is my address and telephone number and I pray that no matter what happens, whether this letter has reached my father or not, that I will receive some sort of reply, positive or negative. This would make my holiday season the greatest I could ever dream of.

Hopefully,

Harold Handley English

It was just a coincidence that I had sent that letter during National Adoption Week ... or was it? A month went by, then two months, with no return word, so I assumed that was that. It was just another of many dead ends.

About three months after I sent the letter, I came home from work and fished the mail out of the mailbox as usual. As I was thumbing through the bills and catalogs, I came across a thick envelope with a return address of Vernon and Rachel Handley from somewhere called Stroud, Oklahoma.

Oh my God, Vernon Handley? Could that be my Vernon Lee Handley? And how about the name Rachel, my daughter's name is Rachael...coincidence?

I walked as fast as I could to the kitchen table—actually, I ran—and I tore open the side of the thick envelope. Polaroid snapshots spilled out all over the table, and while I was wondering who these people were, I pulled out a letter:

Dear Harold,

My name is Vernon Lee Handley and I was married to a German citizen, Elisabeth Stapf. We had three sons who were adopted in 1964 by a Harrison F. English of Trenton, NJ.

Some of my background is as follows. I served in the U.S. Army for approximately thirty years, retiring September 1, 1975 from Ft. Leavenworth, Kansas. I now live on a small farm in Oklahoma (the state in which I was born), about fourteen miles out in the country near Stroud, Oklahoma. During the year I drive a school bus for the school district, which gives me time for work and ranching.

Needless to say I was very surprised to receive your letter. I had almost given up hope of ever hearing or seeing any of my three older sons. I have received much encouragement from my family that I answer your letter. Since they were old enough to understand, the children have known that they have three older brothers, a fact that I have never denied. I do not understand why your mother felt it necessary to conceal my identity.

I am happy to learn of your wife and daughter and wish them well. Your letter did not say what you do or any information about the rest of the family. I hope to receive a reply.

I am truly sorry that your search for me has been so long and difficult. I have had no reason to keep my whereabouts from anyone. From your letter you sound like a very mature, caring and understanding person. I am happy that you persisted in your search all of these years.

I hope this letter finds everyone well. Perhaps we can get more details of one another in the future. I am enclosing some pictures of my family (please excuse the expression on my face as these are only proofs).

Again, I want to say that I was very happy to receive your letter. If you have any specific questions please let me hear from you. I would like for you to know that I have always loved you boys and that I will always have a special place in my heart for each of you.

Love Always,

Vernon Handley

P.S. Your sister did this letter on a computer at school. She wanted to have a part.

I couldn't believe what I was reading. I just sat there frozen and staring at all the pictures. There were pictures of a family I never knew. I discovered that I had two half-sisters and two half-brothers who were twins. There were photos of aunts and uncles, and then the most important prize of all, a picture of my father.

As I read the letter for the umpteenth time, I thought that he was just as aloof in his letter as I had been in mine. I assumed that he didn't know whether I wanted to pursue a relationship or if was looking for general information.

Armed with my letter and an incredible feeling of happiness and excitement, I called my wife. Next I called the congressman's staffer and gave her the good news. Later that night, after talking it over with my family, I decided I had to tell my older brothers, even though I hadn't seen or spoken to either of them in many years. How could I have further contact with my father or even meet him without them?

It was going to be a tough thing to do, but it was the right thing to do. It was that damned Huck Finn inside of me—he was always making me do the right thing. This revelation was going to affect them and their children forever, so it had to be done.

I met with both of my older brothers that night, and I told them that I had found our father, and I wasn't talking about Harrison's ghost. I threw the pictures and the letter down on the coffee table and watched their reactions.

For what seemed like an eternity there was nothing but dead silence and awkward, disbelieving stares. Finally, my brothers began picking up the pictures with their trembling hands and each took a turn reading the letter. I never expected the reaction I got from one brother, because he had always been adamant about not searching for our father.

He had declared years before that he didn't care who or where our father was. He felt that our father had deserted us, as he'd always been told by our mother. She had told him that our father was abusive toward both her and us. When I had first asked him to help me find our father, his answer was that Dad gave us up for adoption and didn't care about us, so why should we give a darn about him?

His response surprised me also because of all the crap that I had taken from him all those years. He started crying—I mean, really crying. He took off his glasses because he had to wipe the tears from his eyes and couldn't see. Old habits die hard, I guess, because he then called me a creep for making him cry.

So now they knew what I knew—Dad was alive and well and lived in a small town in Oklahoma, he was married to Rachel, and we had two younger half-brothers and two younger half-sisters who had known about us all of their lives. There were no secrets on the Handley side of the family. We had aunts and uncles strewn all over the Midwest who had known all about us these entire thirty-five years of separation.

It is difficult to explain the strong sense of accomplishment and pride that came over me after I told them both the news that night.

By the time I left my brother's house, they had decided they were each going to answer Dad's letter with one of their own, complete with pictures of their children, and tell him all about their own families. We all became regular pen pals with Dad for the next few months.

It's funny how the mind works and I can't explain the reason why, but that night I took my tri-fold adoption papers and tucked them into the handwritten envelope that my father used to send his first letter to me. To this day that's where they still are, safely nestled inside his envelope with the return address of Vernon and Rachel Handley, Stroud, Oklahoma. It somehow felt and seemed right.

CHAPTER SIXTEEN

PHONE CALL

Our father was planning to visit us in New Jersey, and after several months of letters back and forth, the three of us boys met again to plan the visit. Finally we decided that enough was enough, and we should just call him.

We arranged to hook up a telephone with a speaker, and we set up a tape recorder next to it to record our first conversation with our father. This was the first time in our lives that we three boys had ever done anything together.

"OK, guys, it's time to get on with it and dial the number," said my older brother. "Hal, you found him, so why don't you speak first?"

I was being treated as an equal by my brother for the first time in my life. And he had even called me Hal, acknowledging that I was a new person and not the old Harold my brothers used to know.

We dialed the phone and turned on the tape recorder. Our youngest half-sister answered the phone. She had just graduated from high school and was studying at Oklahoma Baptist University at the time.

"Sis, this is your brother Hal here. Is Dad home?"

"Ahhhh!" she screamed. "He's not here right now, its bowling league night in Stroud."

Stroud is a tiny town in central Oklahoma right off of the Turner Turnpike in between Oklahoma City and Tulsa. It now has two claims to fame, both of which came a few years later. First, a young woman from little Stroud won the Miss America contest, and second, a huge shopping outlet center was built in town. The outlet center created a lot of jobs, but it was destroyed in a tornado just a couple of years later devastating the town.

Our sister told us that he'd be back in an hour or so and that he would be excited to get our phone call. Later we learned that she had called her mother, Rachel, at the bowling alley to make sure Dad went straight home and didn't stop for coffee and a piece of pie, which is what one usually did on a night out in Stroud. Rachel got him home without mentioning the call so we could surprise him.

We called again and turned on the tape recorder, and after much fumbling around, we finally connected to Oklahoma and Rachel, Dad's wife.

Rachel: "Hello, Who's this?"

"Hi, this is the boys. OK, could you hang on for a minute? I want to put you on speakerphone. How are you doing tonight?"

Rachel: "I'm just fine, which one is this?"

"Yes, yes, we're all sitting around the table, and I just put you on a speakerphone so we can all talk and hear."

Rachel: "OK, um, um, I'm going to put your daddy on. Here comes your daddy. OK."

After a long, pregnant pause: "Hello." His voice was very deep, and he obviously was nervous.

"Hi Dad, how are you doing?" I said.

After a long pause, because none of us could find the words, I took over:

"Dad, Dad, this is Hal calling, we're calling to confirm your letter. We want you to know that those dates are all right and that if you need more time, you can have more time. And we want you to get back to us as soon as possible and let us know when you're flying in and what your times are. How are you doing?"

Dad: "I'll be all right in a minute."

"Hang in there, we'll be all right. How was bowling today?"

Dad: "Well, not too well."

"Not too good?" Everybody was laughing.

"Why, what happened?" we asked.

Dad: "Well, there was a reason." He chuckled softly.

"What reason was that? Did you get a call? Did you get a call at the bowling alley, Dad?"

Dad: "Yes I did, they didn't tell me why, but I knew something was up."

"Hey, we're all sitting around listening here on speaker."

Dad: "You guys don't know how and what this is doing to me!"

"Well, Dad, it's doing the same thing to all of us," I said.

Dad: "Gosh, you guys don't know how much this call means to me. I had put you boys in a little box in my heart and threw away the key always hoping and praying that someday you would find me and open it."

Then he said the words that made me the proudest I'd ever been in my life:

"I'm so thankful to Harold for keeping up with his search for me all those years."

"Well, that's Harold," said my older brother. "He's a bulldog."

"I have to give my wife, Diane, a lot of credit for this too; she made a lot of connections for me to do it," I said. "And Sis sounds real nice; I think we threw her for a loop."

Dad: "She's my pride and joy, that's the baby, that's Daddy's baby!"

"She was a little surprised when we called," I said.

Dad: "I imagine she was. I was surprised when Rachel told me that you guys had called."

"Well, we've been waiting for a little while now and we figured it was time to stop these letters and get down to it, you know."

Dad: "Oh, that last letter that I wrote. That took me a couple of weeks to write it. I can tell you boys a whole lot of things once we get face to face and get the preliminaries out of the way. We can't wait... well I can't wait to see you guys."

"Yeah, that's for sure," we chimed in. "You guys are welcome to come up and stay for as long as you want, you know."

Dad: "Oh, I know that, son." It was the first time he'd used the word "son," and boy, it felt good. "But we've got to go to California, too, for your brother who is being released from the military. We're going to drive out from here. The base is in California and he gets home in September."

"When in September?"

Dad: "Oh, well, his release from the army is I believe the fourteenth of September, but it takes about a week to get from home to San Diego."

"So when can we expect you in New Jersey?"

Dad: "Be the last week in July, the boys have a birthday on July thirtieth so we have to be back, they're twins, you know."

"Oh yeah, we got that from the letters."

Dad: "So just before you guys called, your brother called and Rachel told him about this, so now when we finish talking I've got to call him, ha, ha, ha."

At this point in the call, we could hear Dad yawn.

"You must be tired, Dad," I said. "We forgot about the time zone change."

Dad: "Yeah. If you guys are anything like me you need your beauty sleep, ha, ha, ha. Ahhh, it's just so great to hear from you boys and we would like to come to New Jersey on the twenty-seventh."

"Good, sold," we replied.

Dad: "I can't explain it, but I have to meet you boys' right where I left you, in New Jersey. It's something that I just have to do. We're going on Monday to get our tickets. Is Philadelphia all right with you? Because that way we only have one change to make instead of two."

Well, listen guys, like I said in my letters, it's just been so many years and so much heartache too. I suffered a long, long time, and it's all coming back to me now all at one time. I am truly sorry and don't know why I had to be kept a secret from all you children. Harold, you share a special birthday with me, and someday I'll tell you why. I'm a diabetic, I have to take insulin and I'm doing pretty well, but stress raises my blood sugar and I have to be very careful."

"How long has that been going on?"

Dad: "The insulin, about two years and maybe fifteen years or so as a diabetic, but I was able to control it with diet until a couple of years ago. It went out of control and they put me on MPH, mild insulin. But I'm all right, I can do almost anything, but I have to stay away from stress and this is definitely stressful!"

"Sorry about that, Dad," we all chimed in, laughing.

Dad: "I was hoping that you guys, in some way, would get together and call me because I knew I couldn't talk to all three of you separately ... I just couldn't ... it probably wouldn't work." Dad started crying and couldn't speak any longer.

I jumped in saying "Dad, Dad, we're going to cut it off and hang up now, just call and let us know what your flight plans are and we'll do the rest. It was great talking to you after all these years. Goodbye."

We never did get to meet Dad for the first time in New Jersey because we had to pick him up from the airport in Philadelphia, but for him, it was close enough.

There we all finally were, at long last. My brothers and I and our wives were waiting at Philadelphia International Airport for the passengers who had just landed from Oklahoma. Passenger after passenger walked by until finally he strode out. I could pick him out of a crowd because I had been studying his picture every day since the day I had opened the envelope he'd sent.

He was a tall, burly man, and I could just tell that he had worked hard all of his life. He was sporting both a military baseball cap and a close-cropped army issue haircut peeking out from under the sides. His wife, Rachel, accompanied him. She was tall and thin and very good-looking, though her face showed the telltale signs of wear from years as a Midwestern rancher's wife. I learned to love Rachel quickly, almost instantly.

I was first to reach him, and I held out my hand to shake his. This big guy just batted my hand away and said, "No handshake here." He proceeded to give me a big bear hug and a kiss on the cheek.

The strange feelings that rushed over me were like nothing I had experienced before or have felt since. The only way to describe it is to say that it felt like someone had thrown a bucket of ice water over me from head to toe. I was drenched, and the emotion was incredible, but what was this new sensation?

Quickly, I realized what the response was, and it caught me by surprise. It was those wonderful, strong feelings of love people naturally have for their parents. All my life I'd thought there was something seriously wrong with me because I'd never had nor understood those emotions in others. I thought back to the night my stepfather died and how I didn't have any feelings for him at all.

Until now, I'd never known what these emotions were or how powerful they were. *Oh my God* this was my father. I was actually hugging my real father and feeling the love for him from the very first second of meeting him. Amazingly, I felt whole for the first time in my life. I learned right then that it doesn't matter how old you are or how far you have come in life. When you see your father for the first time, you are a child again, even for that brief moment. I wanted to break down crying but choked back the tears. It wasn't the proper time and place for sadness, this was a joyous occasion.

In the car on the way to my house my dad said "While we don't have very much of a past, I am eternally grateful that we now have a future."

We had a great few days of visiting and catching up. I had a homecoming party at my house, and we had a cake decorated with a picture of a heart on it, complete with a door and a key in the lock. The image on the cake showed the key had been turned sideways and the door in the heart was now wide open. Dad took notice of it immediately and said that was the sweetest and most wonderful cake he have ever seen or eaten. Even being a diabetic, he had to dive in.

The congressman and his staffer both came to the homecoming party. Dad was excited to meet them and thanked them both for going above and beyond the call of duty and reuniting our family. They presented my father and me with an American flag that was flown over the United States Capitol building in Washington D.C. in honor of the reunion of the Handley family. The flag came with a signed and numbered certificate that read, "This is to certify that the accompanying flag was flown over the United States Capitol on June 4, 1986.... presented to the Handley family"

My dad cried when he was presented with that flag for two reasons. He said the first reason was because of our reunion after thirty-five years apart, and the second reason was that he was

American military through and through, and he was gratified that a United States Congressman had taken the time to have that that flag fly over the U.S. Capitol in honor of our family reunion.

I realized that day that if you cut into my dad with a scalpel, he would bleed red, white and blue. That flag meant the world to him. My stepmother, Rachel, presented it to me when Dad passed away fifteen years later. The flag is in my possession now, and it means the whole world to me, too. It's one of my most prized possessions.

Throughout our reunion Dad never spoke in a negative way about our mother. That positive approach endeared him to me even more, but now the fragments of the puzzle began fitting together. Revelations pieced together during that weekend, and other stories I heard during several conversations with my dad, finally revealed all of the details of the dirty secret of the English clan, and why they had to be kept hidden from the world. Well, at least once again in my life I thought I had learned all of the secrets.

Two humorous stories came out of our first weekend together. The first was that upon receiving the first letter from me via the army, my dad couldn't bring himself to open it. He was afraid of it. He was afraid that I was writing a letter to tell him off for leaving us children, or to tell him that I hated him for it.

When he first received my letter, his wife Rachel placed it on their dining room hutch, where it stayed unopened for three months, but not untouched. Every couple of days Dad would pick it up, hold it to the light, and pace around the room staring at it, but he couldn't bring himself to open it. He always set it back in place on the hutch.

One day Rachel decided she'd had just about enough of that, so she got out her tea kettle and carefully steamed open the envelope. I'll always love her and be grateful to her for that. She read the letter and secretly shared it with her children. Then she glued it back together and put it back on the hutch as though nothing had changed.

When my Dad came home that day and went through his now normal routine of picking it up and staring at it, she said, "Listen, you have to either open the mail or I'm throwing it away, but it cannot sit there any longer." That's when Dad finally opened the letter, and that's the reason it took him three months to answer.

The other funny story was that when my dad was serving in Vietnam, he knew that we three boys were coming of age for the military draft and would probably be there with him at some point soon. He was a master sergeant and was placed in charge of procurement and supplies in Vietnam. Anything that came over from the United States for the soldiers had to go through him, at least on paper. He was in charge of all the mail, supplies, guns, ammo, the food—everything. Each time a new set of draftees came over, my dad would pore over the list looking for our names. He just knew at least one of us would be there someday, and although Vietnam was a horrid place and he didn't wish it on anyone, he couldn't wait for one of us to show up.

One night as he was looking over the daily roster of new soldiers coming in, up popped a familiar name: Harold English. He couldn't believe his luck. He'd finally found me, halfway around the world in a hellhole, but he'd found me. He paced around his camp for hours but he couldn't sleep, and he couldn't wait for morning to come. He got into his Jeep that night and drove straight through the Vietnam jungle to the place where Harold was stationed.

He woke the sergeant in charge and demanded to see Harold English immediately despite it being four o'clock in the morning. The sergeant, being of lower rank, immediately went and rousted Harold from his bunk and marched him in front of my dad. The only problem was that Harold was a young black soldier, and he obviously was not me. Another dead end!

My dad, Harold, and the sergeant had a good laugh when he explained the story, and Dad took Harold out to breakfast and apologized for waking him up.

One day I'm going to find that Harold English and tell him our story, and I'll share the laugh with him, too.

CHAPTER SEVENTEEN

REUNITED

We boys finally decided that we were going to bring our families to Oklahoma to meet all the other relatives. We had uncles, aunts, half-brothers and half-sisters that we still hadn't met. It was a fantastic trip that I'll never forget. I still have a videotape of us all telling stories, laughing and playing like a true family on the front lawn of my dad's small ranch in Stroud, Oklahoma.

Stroud is a typical worn-down old Midwestern town that at one time was booming with railroad and oil workers. Back in the old days, cowboys and Indians roamed everywhere. Founded in 1892, Stroud was populated by early settlers who'd arrived the good, old-fashioned way—by wagon train.

Back then, the original Indian Territory surrounding the town was "dry," but the sale of alcohol was permitted in Stroud, so it became quite the hot spot for the likes of Jessie James, the Dalton brothers, and Wyatt Earp, all of whom at one time hung both their hats and their six guns there.

Now, downtown looks like a ghost town to me. It is almost completely abandoned, with a rapidly shrinking population. However, in 2005, Stroud was recognized as the grape and wine capital of Oklahoma, with fifteen wineries within fifty miles. Any town with that much wine can't be all bad.

It looked like the old tired town was rode hard and put away wet. Its main street served as the Ozark Trail, and it is part of the famous and historic Route 66 highway. The busiest building in town is, by no mistake, the church. This is after all, the Bible belt.

At the town border, a sign welcomes visitors. It doesn't say, "Welcome to Stroud, Oklahoma: Our People Are Americana Personified," but it certainly should.

Stroud's citizens are a proud bunch—very proud of their country and of the American military. Almost every Stroud family has deep military roots going back generation before generation. You can just see and feel Mom and Pop, apple pie, and patriotism everywhere in this old Midwestern town. You can also sense the friendliness and honesty of its steadfast, hardworking people.

Everywhere you go you are greeted with a smile and a friendly, laid-back, "How ya'll doin' today?" Stroud is very different from the East Coast and my New Jersey home. In fact, it's not just different, it's exactly the opposite, and I loved it.

The Handley reunion made the local Oklahoma newspaper, *The Stroud American,* and also the local General Motors newspaper where I worked at the time, *The Trenton Tribune.*

The Stroud American Kendrick News ran an article titled *Father and Family Reunited after Many Years.* In the article the author wrote that Vernon Handley received word from the Armed Services that his sons were trying to locate him through military channels. The article spelled out our history. It stated that Vernon hadn't seen his children since he left for war in Korea in 1952 thirty five years ago. The story even announced that his wife had divorced him and taken the children. What it didn't mention was that it was done illegally and without his knowledge, he still wouldn't speak negatively.

The Trenton Tribune ran a front page story titled *A Very Special Christmas Gift* by Jim Sahol. It read "Christmas is a traditional time of giving. This year one of our employees will be getting something very special – a gift which won't be under the tree. Hal English will be spending his first Christmas with his natural father. Separated at six months old, Hal never knew he was adopted until finding some documents sixteen years ago. Since that time, he has been writing letters all over the country trying to locate him. Persistence paid off, and through the military, he finally found him. A letter arrived from Oklahoma which opened a whole new world – a father, two sisters, twin brothers, and countless other relatives who are anxious to meet him face to face. So if Hal seems to be smiling a lot more than usual these days, it is because his Christmas gift is one money can't buy as he travels to Stroud, Oklahoma to receive the gift of family."

At our reunion the whole Oklahoma clan agreed that my father and I were so much alike that it was scary. We had the same personality, the same sense of humor, the same sense of being, and even some of the same mannerisms. It's no wonder that Harrison hated and abused me so much. It turned out that I was the persona of Vernon Lee Handley right in his face, taunting him every day of his life; I just didn't know it.

The Handley family was now put back together and complete and things were back in the right order ... almost. We had just one more thing to do and one more reunion to go which happened one year later.

The next year while my wife, Diane, was expecting with our second child, Christopher, we were planning the baby's christening at our local church. It presented a big problem, as my father was very religious and wanted to come to New Jersey for the event. The dilemma was, so did my mother. This confused me a little, because she wasn't religious at all, and Mom knew that Vernon would be coming. My brothers and I talked about it extensively. We were all afraid something would happen and one of them would say something nasty. And who could blame them? I knew at the time it wouldn't be my Dad because he was a good man and above any negative reactions.

At that point, I had grown to know my father well. I also knew that he would never do anything to upset me or my family. My biggest fear was that since he had recently undergone open-heart surgery, this reunion might cause something bad to happen to his heart. There was no way I could ask him or my mother not to come. As I look back, I realize it could have been, and probably should have been, a very ugly scene.

Fortunately for me, I lived in a split-level home with a large great room downstairs and a formal living room upstairs. My father flew into New Jersey that morning, and my older brothers picked him up to let him know that our mother, Elizabeth, would be there.

I was never more proud of Dad than when he marched right

into my house after the church service, went straight downstairs, and strolled directly up to my mother.

"Hello, Elizabeth," Dad said as he shook my mother's hand. Mom just stayed in her seat with a blank look on her face and shook his hand, uttering a chilling, "Hello, Vernon." That was it, "Hello." After all those years and all that trouble, just, "Hello." It wasn't very much, but at least it was some kind of closure.

There was a pregnant pause in the room. No one knew what to say or what to expect from the reunion of these two after all the years, after all of the lies and deceit. My dad turned around, and I accompanied him upstairs into the living room to have some refreshments and to hold his newly christened grandson for the first time. My two older brothers then ushered him out and took him to one of their houses for the rest of his weekend in New Jersey.

After all Elizabeth had done to him and to us, he was a proud Midwestern gentleman to the end. It was the one and only time we kids ever would see our parents together in the same room. It was the last time they would ever see each other as well.

CHAPTER EIGHTEEN

TRUTH WILL OUT

Dad had signed up for military service at a young age and was a lifer in the army. He served for two tours in Korea and two tours in Vietnam. I later found out that he was an E8 master sergeant and that the army had created that E8 rank specifically for him. He had lacked the college education needed to become an officer, yet he was an amazing soldier and a natural leader of men.

His family, our family now, were proud dirt farmers from way back. In fact, his grandfather's claim to fame was that the Dalton gang once rode up to his horse farm and at gunpoint stole four of his best ponies. They left behind the overtired horses they'd stolen from the rancher just one town over. Another bit of family lore claims that the Handley's are distantly related to Wyatt Earp.

The first of the Handley clan to come to this country was Virgil Vernon Handley, my father's grandfather. Virgil entered the country in a way that was not too unusual for the 1800s. As a young man, he stowed away on a ship coming from his native Ireland. He came for the promise of an American way of life. That was my great-grandfather, who later became a stonemason and settled down in Missouri.

It's interesting to me that I carry the last name of English, but I am actually half Irish. 'Tis a mad Leprechaun's curse, to be sure!

Great Granddad Virgil was a ladies' man, just like my dad. He would swim everyday across a river in Missouri to court the farmer's daughter across the water. The Handley folklore says he would strip down and tie his clothes into an oilcloth pouch so they wouldn't get wet. Then he would swim across with the pouch balanced on his head and put his clothes back on once he reached the other side. After a short courtship, the farmer's daughter consented to marry him to save him from drowning because he wasn't a very good swimmer. At least, that's how the Handley tale goes. As a stonemason, he helped build many historic and important buildings throughout the Midwest.

After retiring from the army, my dad purchased a small ranch in the middle of Stroud, a no man's land where he was raising about thirty head of cattle. His first letter to me said that he didn't know why it was such a secret who he was or where he was all of these years. His children in Oklahoma knew about us three boys their entire lives. He also, much to his credit, said he had no desire to talk in a bad way about our mother, but that he would share the history of what had happened as he knew it. Finally, more of the pieces to the puzzle I was trying to piece together began to fit into place.

Back in 1947, my dad was a young man who enlisted in the army after he'd failed to amount to anything in Oklahoma. He said he enlisted to stay out of trouble and maybe to keep him out of jail, where he might have wound up.

He was stationed in Stuttgart, Germany, for a period of time, as were many young American GIs. One day he was patrolling the area by driving around in his army Jeep, and he saw a young, beautiful German girl walking down the street near the local hospital. That hospital had been taken over by the US Army during the occupation. In 1947, the American army had just lifted the rule prohibiting contact between soldiers and German citizens that had been instituted at the time of occupation in 1945 and 1946.

Dad, like the stud he thought he was, pulled over and offered this cutie a ride. I'm surprised he didn't offer her nylons and chocolate or cigarettes, but then again, maybe he did. Cigarettes were the desired form of currency on the German black market, much like they were back at home in the Trenton Madhouse. With cigarettes, you could buy anything you needed or wanted, especially if they were the better American brand cigarettes.

That young woman was Elizabeth, my mother. She accepted the ride home, hopped into the Jeep and started flirting with my father like crazy. She told him her name was Elizabeth Stapf and that she was working at the hospital. She was all alone and lonely, as she had lost all of her friends and most of her family during the bombings. Dad was mesmerized by her stories and her seeming vulnerability and was immediately smitten with her.

They began dating and had a whirlwind romance. They would drive the German countryside in the Jeep and picnic at some of the most scenic places my dad had ever seen. My mother would supply a beautifully packed picnic basket and a bottle of homemade wine. They spent almost every Sunday for months sitting on a blanket, drinking wine, eating cheese and bread and making love.

Things progressed quickly, and Elizabeth got pregnant, and so they had to get married. During her pregnancy, my mother kept working at the hospital every day, up until the day she had the baby.

About a year or so after the birth of their son, my father got stationed in the United States at Ft. Knox, Kentucky, for a couple of years. There, my other brother, who was conceived in Germany, and I were born. My brother's birthday in the United States was uneventful. My birthday a year and half later was something altogether different.

My mother was nine months along in her pregnancy with me and my dad was at work at the base when it was time for me to make my entrance into the world. She phoned my dad, who then called the army base hospital and gave them the address of the barracks, telling them she was about to break water and have the baby.

An hour went by, and no one came. My mother was having contractions and was about to have the baby. She called my dad again to tell him she was still at home, yet no ambulance had come.

Dad jumped into his Jeep and raced home. He picked up my mother and carried her to the Jeep and sped off to the hospital. As he got about halfway to the hospital, my mother's water broke, and she started screaming, "The baby's coming out!" Dad pulled over and ran around the Jeep, catching me just as I came out of the womb screaming like a banshee. He placed me on her lap and rushed to the hospital, where the base doctor took care of the rest.

Later, my parents found out that the original ambulance had gone to the wrong barracks, and the emergency responders were told by a neighbor that it must be a false alarm or a prank call because they knew of no pregnant women living there. That ambulance went back to the base hospital and didn't report anything.

After an internal investigation of the incident, the officer in charge of the hospital was busted down a rank for not having proper procedures in place to report false alarms. We even made the front page of the army newspaper, *The Army Times*. It appears that I came into this world with a big bang and caused trouble from the beginning. Sorry, Colonel, I did not mean to get you busted.

It was 1952, and I was a couple months old when my dad got his papers to report for a tour of duty in the Korean War. He was ordered to report for duty within a few weeks. He showed the orders to his wife and told her he was arranging for her and us three boys to be looked after by his parents in Oklahoma. He said he would take us there, and his family would care for us.

That was when life began to get weird for my dad and our lives changed forever.

Mom showed him a newspaper clipping she had from a city called Trenton, New Jersey. She had an apartment already circled in red ink on the page that she had picked out for us to live in. This confused and infuriated Vernon and started a series of huge arguments. The arguments weren't just between my mother and my father. There were also arguments between my father and his parents and brothers and sisters in Oklahoma who wanted us to be there with family, where they felt we belonged while he was away in Korea.

My father was gravely concerned about leaving his wife and three very young children in a town on the East Coast some fifteen hundred miles away from Oklahoma and his family. My dad's parents, brothers and sisters were a close-knit clan and couldn't believe that we weren't all coming home as a family while Dad went off to war. No one ever understood it, nor could they make any sense of it.

As my father had to ship out to Korea immediately, my mother won the argument. She told him her only living relative in the United States lived in Hopewell, New Jersey, right outside of Trenton. She said her cousin had helped her pick out the apartment, and he would be looking after us while Dad was gone. Dad didn't know that in the 1950s, Hopewell might as well have been on another planet than Trenton because there was no way to get from one town to the other without a car. Hopewell and Trenton were about forty miles apart with no public transportation in between them.

But time was running short for Vernon, so he took us all to Trenton, left us in the apartment my mother and her cousin had picked out, and then hopped a train cross-country and reported for duty in Korea.

Months went by while my dad was serving in the Korean War. His military paychecks were mailed to the United States and cashed by my mother in Trenton, but his letters weren't being answered. He wrote letter after letter, but still there was no reply. He knew she was receiving the letters because his checks were enclosed and they were being cashed in the United States.

My dad told me this went on for months, causing him enormous stress. He said he couldn't eat, sleep, or think straight, and his only relief turned out to be the bottle.

He started drinking to ease his worries about his wife and children who were all alone in a strange town far away from his family and even farther away from him. He drank so much he became an alcoholic. He would check the army mail call every day, and when there was no letter from Mom, he'd hit the bottle again. He wasn't particular about what he drank; anything he could find would suffice.

Vernon reported to a second lieutenant in Korea, and the lieutenant called him in one day after months of him being drunk on a daily basis. Dad was told he was being sent to rehabilitation. The second lieutenant said, "Vernon, you can drink yourself to death for all I care, but you will no longer endanger the lives of the men serving under you in this war." He knew from my dad's military record that he was a tough soldier and a good, experienced leader. He also knew that with a military record as good as my dad's, it wasn't just the war that was causing the drinking.

My dad broke down and told him the story. He told the lieutenant how he'd had to leave his wife, who was from Germany, and his three young sons in Trenton, New Jersey. He told him Trenton was halfway across the country from his family in Oklahoma, and that he hadn't heard a word from his wife since. He told him the paychecks he was sending were being cashed, but that none of his letters or phone calls had been answered.

The officer said that while my father was in rehabilitation, he would research what was going on in Trenton and find out whatever news he could. He said he knew that Trenton would have a Red Cross station and that he would contact them for help.

Rehabilitation in Korea during wartime wasn't what it is in the United States today. The patients who were addicted to alcohol and drugs were strapped down on a gurney in a hospital ward and made to go through painful withdrawal.

After the withdrawal was done, several of the alcoholics were confined to a large holding cell together. The cell was tiled from ceiling to floor. There was a hole in the center of the floor with an iron grate covering it, and another small hole in the middle of the door.

A hospital staffer would wheel in food and drinks on a cart and leave the cart in the room. My dad couldn't believe his luck. The drinks were alcoholic, and anything he could ask for was on the cart. My dad surmised that the army thought if the men drank nonstop, they would cure themselves after they'd had enough.

Problem was, the booze had been chemically doctored. All of the alcohol was spiked with some substance that made them violently sick. The men started heaving all over themselves and each other. My dad said it was the vilest smelling and most disgusting scene imaginable. After a couple of hours of this, they all stripped off their smelly clothes and threw them in a corner.

There they stood, quite a sight, these brave soldiers, sickly and in their underwear. Finally the little hole in the door opened and a fire hose nozzle was stuck through it. The entire room was doused with ice-cold water. Once the floor was clean, the door opened and staff came in and took the wet, foul-smelling clothes, leaving the men dry clothes and some clean towels.

A few hours passed, and someone wheeled in another cart stocked with the same libations as before. No one said a word to the men; they just left the cart. Hungry and thirsty, one by one they started eating the food, but some did not drink the alcohol on the cart. Those, including my dad, who did drink repeated the same disgusting scene again and again until they couldn't even look at a bottle without the urge to throw up. Those who learned their lesson and didn't touch it were let go, rehabilitated.

Dad got out a few weeks later and reported to the lieutenant who had sent him into rehab. The lieutenant told him that he had some good news but also some bad news. He told my dad that his wife and children were fine. The officer had been in contact with the American Red Cross in Trenton and had correspondence that the three children were well.

He said that Elizabeth was having some minor problems dealing with being alone in the United States and was under the care of a doctor. He told Vernon that it wasn't a big deal and that everything was expected to be fine. The lieutenant advised my dad to keep having his paychecks sent to her but not to look for letters as there wouldn't be any for a while, at least until she got better. He sent Dad back to the war with nothing but worry on his mind and a Red Cross letter in his hand.

Several months later, Vernon got an extended leave between his tours of duty, and he came back to Trenton looking for his wife and children. He wrote one last letter to his wife telling her of his arrival plans. Writing that letter and giving her advanced notice of his arrival turned out to be one of the biggest mistakes of his life, of our lives.

Vernon got into Trenton by train late at night, right on schedule. He took a cab to the apartment where he had left us months before and knocked on the door. There was no answer, so he knocked louder. There was still no answer, so he started banging on the door. A neighbor came out and told him that no one lived there anymore. "They moved out about a week ago," he said. "I don't know where they went." Dad asked if it was a German woman with three children, and the neighbor said yes, and that one of them was just a baby. That would have been me.

After hearing this news, my dad didn't know what to do. As it was late at night, he decided to sleep on the porch. Ironically, I would do the same thing in that same neighborhood sixteen years later.

The next day, he took a cab to my mother's cousin's farm in Hopewell, thinking we had to be there. No such luck. When Dad arrived at the farm, Uncle Art, as we called him, ushered him in and asked him to have a seat at the kitchen table at the old farmhouse. "Sit, down Vernon," my uncle said solemnly. "I have something to show you." Without another word, Uncle Art pulled out a newspaper, folded it to the classified section and pointed to the segment titled "Wedding Announcements." There, staring Vernon in the face, was an announcement of the marriage of Harrison Force English to Elizabeth Stapf.

My father was dumbfounded. How could this possibly be?

Uncle Art explained that all he knew about it was that Harrison and Elizabeth met, fell in love, and got married. He explained that the children were fine but that when Elizabeth got Vernon's letter saying he was coming to New Jersey, she had taken the children and hidden them away. Uncle Art said he knew this because she and Harrison had asked him to help hide the children. Art had refused to have any part of it. He tried to convince Vernon that wherever the children were hidden, he would never be able to find them. Uncle Art gave his condolences and advised my dad to go back to the war and then home to Oklahoma forever. He said there was nothing Vernon could do about it because Elizabeth didn't want to see him anymore, and that Harrison's family was very powerful and could cause trouble for everyone.

My father was incensed at this revelation, and he was not a guy you would want to get angry. He was a big man, about six foot two, and thanks to the military, he was in the best shape of his life. After digesting the devastating news from Uncle Art, he walked from the farm in Hopewell halfway to Trenton before hitching a ride. All that time, he kept wondering where he had heard the name Harrison English before. He was sure it was a familiar name, but where had he heard it?

While sitting in the train terminal, irate about this newest disclosure and waiting for the next train out of Trenton, it finally dawned on him. That name—Harrison English. It was in the Red Cross letter.

Vernon pulled the folded letter out of his uniform pocket and couldn't believe his eyes. There, in the last paragraph of the letter, it said that Elizabeth was fine but under the care of a psychiatrist. That psychiatrist's name was Dr. Harrison F. English. That's where he'd heard the name before. It had been right in his pocket the entire time.

He went to a phone booth and picked up a phone book, finding a home address and phone number for a Dr. Harrison and Rhoda English listed in Morrisville, Pennsylvania. He also found a listing for Dr. Harrison English's office on State Street in downtown Trenton. Vernon tore out the page and asked the station ticket clerk if he knew where State Street was. It turned out the address was only about three miles from the train station. Fuming and with his adrenaline pumping, he ran the three miles to the office.

Harrison's office on State Street was directly across the street from the New Jersey State Capitol building and the governor's office. His office was in a brownstone that had a waiting room for patients out front separated by two frosted glass doors that led into the doctor's private office.

Vernon stormed into the outer office and up to the grey-haired secretary who was sitting there, and he demanded to see Dr. English. He was an imposing figure and was mad as hell, and he must have scared the heck out of that poor secretary.

The secretary picked up the telephone and mumbled something into it while covering the phone with her cupped hand. My dad couldn't make out what she was whispering, but now he could see some sort of hurried movement in the other room through the frosted glass doors. The secretary said in a nervous and shaky voice, "The doctor is not in right now, and you will have to make an appointment to see him."

My father, hearing this and seeing someone's shadow moving on the other side of the glass, got even angrier that the secretary had just lied to him. He walked behind her desk and tried to open the glass doors, which were locked. He shook the doors and banged on them, with no answer. The secretary ran out of the building into the street screaming, and finally Vernon stepped back and kicked the doors in. The glass shattered everywhere and the thin doors flew off their hinges, one crashing to the floor and the other left dangling on one hinge.

There, cowering behind the desk and just hanging up the telephone was the infamous Dr. Harrison Force English. Vernon marched up to Harrison, grabbed him by his suit jacket, and demanded to know where his wife and children were. What had Harrison done with them?

Harrison wasn't saying a word, although he probably couldn't with the choke hold Vernon had on his collar and tie. My father grabbed Harrison's neck and pinned him against the wall behind the desk while shouting at him to tell him where his wife and children were. "I will kill you with my bare hands if you hurt my family," my father shouted into Harrison's face.

Before Harrison could answer, his twin brother, Fred, scurried into the office. Fred was serving as an assistant attorney general for the state of New Jersey at the time, and he had been directly across the street in the state capitol building. There were reinforcements accompanying Fred in the form of two uniformed and armed New Jersey State Troopers. They were stationed at the statehouse across the street and had gotten there in minutes. That was the telephone call Harrison had made while Vernon was in the waiting room being misdirected and stalled by the secretary.

Seeing his brother and the troopers instantly emboldened Harrison, who stood up, straightened his clothes, and boldly proclaimed, "You don't have a wife and children anymore. They are mine! Elizabeth and the children are mine, and they don't ever want to see you again!"

Harrison looked at his brother and then the troopers and screamed, "Look what this maniac has done! He broke in, destroyed my property, threatened my secretary, physically attacked me, and threatened to kill me. Get him the hell out of here. Arrest him!"

With that, the troopers each took hold of one of my father's arms and dragged him to a police car that was parked out front with two other troopers sitting in it. The four of them shoved my father into the backseat with one trooper on each side and two in the front seat. They waited without saying a word to Vernon for about twenty minutes while Harrison and his brother were inside making phone calls and trying to figure out what they were going to do about this ugly situation.

Harrison had never planned for an incident like this. He had never expected to have a face-to-face confrontation with Vernon Lee Handley. He had never thought he would have to see my father in person, let alone be held menacingly in his iron grasp.

Finally, a calmer Harrison called one of the troopers back into the office for a brief conversation. The trooper came out of the brownstone and, without a word, got into the car and drove around the corner and over the Calhoun Street Bridge, which separated New Jersey from Pennsylvania over the Delaware River.

On the other side of the river, the troopers drove down a path to the bank of the river and stopped the car. They yanked my dad out of the car, and all four of them roughed him up. They dragged him to the edge of the river, where two troopers held him while another punched and kicked him. My dad fell to the ground and got kicked a couple more times until they said to him, "If you weren't wearing that army uniform, you'd be dead right now, floating face down in that river!"

One older trooper who seemed to be in charge of the others pointed across the river and said, "That is New Jersey and this is Pennsylvania. If you ever again in your life cross that river, ever, you will be tried and convicted for the attempted murder of Dr. Harrison English. Do you understand?"

He went on to say that eyewitnesses would testify in court that

Vernon had broken into the good doctor's office, threatened his secretary, attacked him, and attempted to kill him. "We promise you that you will face a quick trial and you will be imprisoned," he said. "Do you understand what we are saying to you, soldier? Do you realize how serious this is and how much trouble you are in?"

All my father could do was say yes. They told him that if he ever came back to New Jersey and was convicted of attempted murder, he would be given a minimum of twenty years to life at hard labor in Trenton State Prison. The troopers got into their car and drove across the bridge to New Jersey and parked on the other side. They watched to see whether Vernon would cross back over the bridge, or if he had gotten their message.

Vernon sat there for a while trying to make sense of everything, but he just couldn't. None of this was logical. After a few minutes he stood up, straightened his uniform, washed the blood off his face in the river, and hitchhiked to the Philadelphia train station. He returned to Korea with both a broken heart and a broken spirit.

Several months later, when Vernon's second tour in Korea was over and he had some time, he came back to Morrisville, Pennsylvania. He remembered that when he had looked up Dr. Harrison English earlier, there were two names and addresses in the phone book and he still had that torn page in his pocket. One was listed as Harrison and Rhoda English with a Morrisville address for his home, and the other was the Trenton address for the office. Since it was in Pennsylvania and not New Jersey, he decided to pay a visit to the Morrisville address and try his luck there.

Rhoda English opened the door of a beautiful brick home overlooking the banks of the Delaware River. The home had a "For Sale" sign on the front lawn. By her side, clinging to her leg was a young girl of about four years old.

When Vernon introduced himself, he was surprised to be invited in for coffee and cake; it wasn't the screaming match he'd expected. That afternoon, Rhoda and Vernon put some of the pieces together. Rhoda told him that she and Harrison were man and wife, and that she was considerably older than Harrison. She explained to my dad that, try as they might, they just couldn't have children. She said the little girl who was now playing in the other room was her niece, and that Rhoda was raising her.

Rhoda told Vernon that Harrison's family was powerful in New Jersey politics. She said Harrison's father was the right hand man to the mayor of Trenton, and that his twin brother was assistant state attorney general. Dad told her he had already met the good attorney.

Rhoda said she had discovered that Harrison was carrying on an affair with my mother. He would leave home every morning, drive over the bridge to his new girlfriend's apartment for a morning tryst, then drive around the corner and down the street to his psychiatric office on State Street. In the evening, he would go back to Elizabeth's apartment for some dinner and then return home for the night to Rhoda and her niece. The problem for Harrison was that he got his girlfriend, my mother, pregnant with my younger brother and that screwed everything up—for him, anyway. That little slip-up ruined both Harrison's convenient trysts and also a lot of lives.

Rhoda was kind to my father that afternoon and told him she would be selling the house and moving to California with her niece. She said Harrison had agreed to pay her half of his income for the rest of his life and that he was never to see or contact Rhoda or her niece again. She warned Vernon not to go back to New Jersey, as the English family were a ruthless bunch and would surely keep their promise of throwing him in jail—or they might even have him killed.

Actually Harrison had a bigger problem than the worry that my father might show up in New Jersey. My mother and Harrison both understood their dilemma, but my father and Rhoda unfortunately did not. My father, Vernon, had in his possession a letter from the American Red Cross, a certified government agency, which identified my now stepfather as a psychiatrist who was professionally caring for a patient named Elizabeth Stapf.

Harrison would have lost everything. His blue-blooded and politically connected family would have faced public embarrassment. He would have lost his license to practice medicine. He would have lost his job at the state psychiatric hospital as well as his private practice. If word of this had gone public, he would have been professionally and personally washed up.

It's no wonder Harrison's people cooked up the attempted murder charge, which my father had conveniently dropped right into their laps. They had to clean up all the loose ends and use all their power and connections, and a good bluff, to do so, or else. Vernon's visit to the doctor's office and the heavy threat of an attempted murder conviction got rid of Vernon Handley once and for all and wrapped up the problem nicely for the English family.

Now, thirty five years later, after all the secrets, lies, and the wastebasket bonfire, the truth had finally come out. A doctor/patient relationship of the kind that they had would have been a huge scandal in the 1950s, especially since it included an illegitimate child. In addition, the doctor had had the affair with a soldier's wife while her husband was away risking his life serving his country at war making it even messier.

CHAPTER NINETEEN

MOM'S STORY

A few months after finding my dad and finally reuniting with him, I confronted my mother with what I knew or at least thought I knew about our seedy family history. I had an insatiable thirst to solve the English/Handley mystery once and for all.

I went to visit my mother at the English Manor for the first time since I had left years earlier. I brought a couple of bottles of her favorite wine with me and told my mother that we had to have a talk. When I walked in, she was sitting in the living room directly underneath the life-sized portrait of Harrison, which was staring down at us.

My mother was in a rare mood that night, especially after a few glasses of the nice German wine I'd strategically brought for the occasion.

I asked her to tell me the whole truth, and I said I wouldn't hold anything against her. I told her that my only regret was that she had not given me the option of growing up with my natural father and his family in Oklahoma instead of living with an abusive stepfather.

I was determined to learn the truth and I guess my demeanor put her at ease, because she actually, for the first and only time, admitted the whole affair to me. She bragged to me that while I had done a good job of putting most of the pieces together, I had missed a few key sections. She decided to enlighten me.

She told me that I wasn't the only abused child in the family. She said she'd been a very poor young girl in Germany with a cruel stepmother who routinely beat her. She was a teenager during World War II and the subsequent Allied occupation of Germany. She said living in Germany during the war was a horror for its citizens, who were all deathly afraid of Hitler and his Nazis, but that the occupation by the Americans was even worse.

She said the Americans came into Germany as a victorious army expecting to continue fighting skirmishes with the citizens while they were occupying the country. What they found surprised them. The German people were a mixed bunch. Most were relieved Hitler was gone and were quite docile, but the American soldiers felt they couldn't be trusted.

The Americans put whole sections of my mother's town off limits to its German citizens. The German families were evicted from their homes with only a few hours' notice. These people were allowed to take only what they could carry, and the Americans didn't care where the people would go or how they would survive. Then the Americans requisitioned—actually, stole—all of the town's supplies, which included local foodstuffs like bread, flour, milk, eggs, potatoes, and vegetables.

My mother told me that when the American GIs first arrived they believed that all of the Germans either committed or supported the atrocities the Nazis had perpetrated at the concentration camps. There was little or no sympathy for the German citizens.

She said the first Americans occupying Germany naturally focused on their own survival needs and not those of the German citizens. They had to quickly repair roads and bridges so supplies and soldiers could come and go. They had to repair the bombed-out railroads, they had to fix the water and sewer utilities, and most important, they had to bury the dead. She said the Americans were so upset and revolted when they saw the death camps, they ordered every German citizen over the age of ten years old to witness the piled-up bodies. They also put the townspeople to work digging graves for the corpses.

The Americans also imposed a non-fraternization rule, which meant that none of the GIs could have personal contact with any of the German people.

Work, however, was another story. The Germans were forced to perform manual labor. It didn't matter if they were doctors, lawyers, teachers, or machinists. They were put to work clearing roads of rubble, burying the dead, and rebuilding the railroads.

My mother said she was put to work peeling potatoes for the soldiers. She peeled thousands of potatoes, but she was grateful for the job because she could hide a few potatoes in her clothes, giving her something to eat at night. She said she was focused solely on her own day-to-day survival.

About a year after the occupation began, the Americans realized that the German citizens wanted no trouble, and the non-fraternization rule was lifted. The Americans started putting the Germans' skills to better use and were finally allowed to intermingle with them. And that's when it started.

At that time, my mother said, Germany had gone wild and was a scary and unsafe place for a young woman like her. Family values gave way to an atmosphere in which people traded sex for food. Crime was rampant, the youth were running wild, and the black market was the only way anyone could buy anything. German women, like my mother, between twenty and thirty years old outnumbered German men three to one. Most of the eligible men had either died in the war or didn't return.

She said every German woman had one thought: survival. Survival in those times meant finding a man to take care of her—preferably an American soldier who could take her away from the madness and hardship of postwar Germany.

When my mother was a mere twenty years old, she was detained by some American GIs. She said she was taken into custody and strip-searched. She was interrogated about a missing GI while standing naked in front of the men. It seemed there were rumors that pretty young German girls were luring unsuspecting GIs with promises of sex, then killing them and stealing their possessions. She managed to convince them she knew nothing about it, and they let her go because the highest ranking soldier felt sorry they had stripped her of her clothes and humiliated her.

She told me she was twenty-two years old when she met my father. At that time, she was starving and alone. She said she'd been lucky enough to get a job working at the hospital in Waiblinger, where she first met Harrison and they fell in love.

Harrison? I laughed and corrected her while filling her glass from our second bottle of wine. I was now very glad that I had brought that German Blue Nun Liebfraumilch wine. Someone told me later that *liebfraumilch* means "mother's milk." How ironic that German mother's milk helped me get the truth out of my mother.

"You mean when you first met Vernon," I corrected her.

She snorted and chuckled while chugging another glass of the wine. "No, I meant what I said, Harrison." She sat there smugly watching the blank and dumbfounded expression on my face.

We both went silent for what seemed like forever while I looked up at Harrison's haunting face in the oil portrait glaring and gloating down at me. I was now confused and I figured the conversation was over and I had been given all the information I was ever going to get.

"You're nuts," I said. "You must be losing it. Here, have some more wine."

She grabbed the bottle out of my hands, stood up and sloppily poured me some more wine, declaring, "Not so, I'm not losing it." Then she said, "Allow me to un-perplex you, my dear Harold."

What she told me next sent shockwaves through my body and brain. It felt as though I were now hooked up to Harrison's electric shock treatment machine and being jolted.

She told me that Harrison English had also been serving in the military and was a doctor and Lieutenant Colonel assigned to that hospital in Germany when the Americans took over during the occupation. They met at the hospital and had a love affair. My mother said she was bowled over by Harrison's stories of the lavish lifestyle that doctors enjoyed in the United States.

They would make love and he would brag of his vacations, parties, and luxuries back home in America. He even boasted to her about a first-class luxury cruise to Liverpool, England, that he had taken.

The problem for my mother was that Harrison was married, a trifling detail he'd left out at first. She said they were madly in love, but then Harrison told her he would have to go back to the United

States without her. Mom said she'd felt she had hit the jackpot meeting Harrison, and she wasn't going to let him go, no matter the cost.

My mother told me she hatched a plan to become an American citizen and get out of poverty forever. She was going to marry Dr. Harrison English somehow, no matter what it took or how long it took. She was going to live that life of luxury and leisure that Harrison had bragged about and enticed her with.

I was stunned at this disclosure. Just when I'd thought I had this mystery figured out, she hit me with this. There was no way I could have ever imagined this scenario.

My mother seemed pleased with herself that I was in a daze over this newest revelation. She went on with her story, slurping the wine like it was water and spilling it on her blouse.

One day, she said, while she was still seeing Harrison, Vernon saw her walking down the street. He pulled up in an army Jeep and offered her a ride home from the hospital. She said she knew instantly that she had just won her ticket to America. She had met a good old country boy who was single, not too bright, and had a heart of gold. She told me she that she instantly knew she could manipulate him and get this soldier to marry her. She turned on the charm and came up with her plan.

She began flirting relentlessly playing damsel-in-distress and reeled my dad into a torrid sexual affair. He fell in love with her. She told me she had never really loved him and was always thinking about Harrison and a pampered life, even when they made love. She deliberately got pregnant as soon as she could so that he would marry her quickly. They had a baby boy.

As she was now married to an American soldier, she became eligible for American citizenship, as did the child. About a year or so later, she got pregnant again, and my dad was assigned to the army base at Ft. Knox, Kentucky. There my other brother was born, followed a year and a half later by my birth in the Jeep.

Continuing her confession, Mom was on a drunken roll. She was clearly enjoying herself while telling me the story she had been covering up for more than thirty years. She kept pouring more wine. I interrupted her and asked her why when Vernon had to go to Korea she had insisted on going to Trenton, New Jersey, instead of to Oklahoma to be with my father's family.

She said she and Harrison were never out of communication with each other. They were always writing letters and calling each other while my father was at work. She told me that when my father got his papers to go to Korea, they realized it was the perfect time to be together.

It was Harrison who'd searched for and found the apartment in Trenton. He'd sent that newspaper to my mother with the apartment circled in red ink. Her cousin from Hopewell was just a ruse, and Vernon never suspected what was really happening.

She declared to me that she'd been determined to marry Harrison and enjoy the wealthy life he'd boasted about. She wanted a life of wealth and privilege so she would never have to be hungry again. She told me that Vernon's entire family had been poor farmers like her family in Germany, and she wasn't going to live that way ever again, not for anyone.

What she didn't know was that although the Handley's were not wealthy, they were rich with something else, love. A love she had never known or understood in her entire life.

That evening, I finally realized exactly how intelligent and devious my mother really was. She had no formal education, but she'd had to be street smart in order to survive the atrocities of war. She'd outsmarted my dad, and later I would find out that she had even outsmarted the Ivy League educated and well-to-do Dr. Harrison Force English.

I asked her what was now heavy on my mind. "Did you blackmail Harrison English into marrying you?"

She laughed and said without hesitation, "Of course I did, and it really wasn't very hard. Harrison was just like every other man I used in my life, always thinking with his private parts. They all become little puppy dogs."

My mother said Harrison was married to an older woman who was unfertile, and Harrison wanted children of his own. She said the sex was great, and once Vernon had left for Korea and she was settled in the apartment in Trenton, they did it every morning before his office hours. This fit perfectly into her long-term plan for Harrison.

It was only a few months before my mother deliberately got pregnant with my half-brother. Once that happened, Harrison was totally ruined.

She said that when she told him they were going to have a child and she wanted him to marry her immediately, he didn't take it very well, he was furious. He started screaming and told her they were through. He said she was nothing but a whore and that he only wanted her to have children, not inherit another wife. He threatened that his family would destroy her, and said he was sending her and her kids to Oklahoma to be with her dirt farmer husband's family. He told her that he had never intended to marry her and that he just wanted her to have his children because his wife, Rhoda, couldn't.

Very seriously, Mom told me that she looked right into Harrison's eyes and said, "I have no intention of going anywhere, Dr. English, ever!"

She asked him if he remembered what they both had told the American Red Cross when they came looking for her. The Red Cross representatives sent by my father from Korea had knocked on the door of her apartment at an opportune time, as Harrison was just leaving after a tryst. When the Red Cross asked how she and the children were and who Harrison was, he made up an answer on the spot. The story that Harrison told them was that he was her doctor and was treating his patient at home for depression. She reminded him that he told the Red Cross it was better to treat her at home because she had three young children and no transportation.

She demanded Harrison now go home to his cozy little family and tell them he knocked up his girlfriend. She said, you will get a quick divorce from your wife and then marry me—no ifs, ands, or buts. If you do not do that, it will be you and your whole family who will be destroyed. You will be the one ruined because by your own official words to the Red Cross you took advantage of me. You, Dr. English, slept with one of your patients every day, sometimes twice a day, until you got her pregnant. You even set her up in an apartment with her three young children so you could screw her while her husband was away serving his country in the war in Korea. Let's see if your precious hoity-toity family likes the scandal. I'll never go to Oklahoma, and you'll go to hell without your medical license, and you will have to pay me support for the rest of my life.

It seems that Harrison had no choice but to comply with everything my mother told him to do for the rest of his life. He had to keep this scandal quiet or face losing the life of luxury he'd so loved and had always crowed about.

I told my mother that night that it was ironic and sad that she'd had to resort to blackmailing Harrison. She was clearly intelligent and talented enough to have come to America on her own like so many other immigrants before her. She could have been anyone she wanted to be without separating the Handley family from its children. She looked at me with distain and declared that she was no immigrant, she was better than that and that she came over to America first class, not steerage.

I now realized that it was no wonder Harrison hated me. He'd been blackmailed into a scandal, a divorce and a new marriage. He was saddled with an about-to-be-born illegitimate son and three other sons who weren't even his. Or on the other hand, weren't they?

Harrison spent thirty two months in Europe and did not leave until after my mother was already married to Vernon Handley. Some have an interesting theory that my two older brothers may in fact be Harrison's sons and not Vernon's, as they both were conceived in Germany while Harrison was there. That could explain why Harrison and Elizabeth always had to keep in touch, even after we went to Ft. Knox, Kentucky. Harrison did tell her he only wanted children, not another wife.

I wonder if that theory would explain the years of abuse and hatred toward only one of the sons—me. I was conceived and born two years after Harrison left Germany and went back home to New

Jersey. Was I the only legitimate son of my mother and Vernon Lee Handley... who knows, it's possible.

It would explain why I am the only son who has all the physical looks, traits and mannerisms of the Handley family. It certainly would explain why my two older brothers are both a good deal shorter than me, as was Harrison. The immediate Handley family members all stand over six feet tall, including the women, as I do. I was the only son who was conceived while my mother was hundreds of miles away from Harrison in Kentucky and he may not have been very happy about that little slip up.

It makes me wonder what other possible reason Harrison would have to keep in touch with my mother after she moved from Germany to Ft. Knox, Kentucky with her husband Vernon and their children. Nothing else makes any sense to me.

Why would Harrison pick out an apartment for my mother to move into in Trenton, N.J. after not seeing her for more than two years?

According to my mother, Harrison wanted children more than anything, but Rhoda couldn't conceive—the exact same story Harrison's first wife Rhoda told Vernon when they met. Was the sex in Germany so good that Harrison couldn't forget it, or did they have the child that Harrison always yearned for, one or two boys keeping them connected for life?

Finally, it could explain why I alone was threatened with commitment to the Trenton Psychiatric Hospital and St. Michael's Orphanage all those years ago.

With my head spinning about my mother's latest revelations, I told her I couldn't understand how she could have divorced my father and married Harrison while my father was serving on the front lines of the war in Korea, without him knowing anything about it or even agreeing to it. How was that even legal?

She said of course it wasn't legal. But the plan she and Harrison cooked up was easy. Harrison got his divorce quickly from Rhoda after agreeing to pay her half of his earnings for the rest of his life.

Then they took a quick trip to Las Vegas, where they found a drunken bum on the street and paid him twenty dollars to stand up in a quickie divorce court. The drunk testified that he was Vernon Lee Handley, signed papers, and agreed to the divorce, with Harrison standing in as a witness.

Afterward, she and Harrison took a stroll down the street to a wedding chapel and got married, with the same drunk standing in as a witness to their wedding. It's a story that could only happen in Las Vegas, after all, what goes on in Vegas, stays in Vegas.

At the time of their illegal divorce and bigamist marriage, my mother was eight months pregnant with Harrison's illegitimate child. Now their secret was safe and all the loose ends were tied up. It was expensive for Harrison, but he was still a doctor, and Elizabeth was now anointed as the queen of the manor. She had finally fulfilled her dream of a life in the lap of luxury, at least for the next few years. And as a bonus, she never ate or peeled a potato again.

My mother was definitely smarter than he was, but Harrison extracted his final revenge about fifteen years later.

In 1970, after spending nine months in the hospital, Harrison lay on his deathbed with no chance of surviving the terrible cancer. Weighing less than ninety pounds, my mother told me that he summoned his best friend, who was also his insurance agent, to his bedside. She said he signed a document canceling all of his insurance, effective that day. He canceled his life insurance, his health insurance—everything.

He left my mother and the children with nothing but a small bank account and the two houses with big mortgages. He left hundreds of thousands of dollars in medical bills. *Touché* Harrison! He had gotten his revenge and left her broke.

In getting his final revenge on my mother for blackmailing him and ruining his life, he sabotaged the future of his own children. The adoption papers I found had declared that Vernon Handley's three boys each had an equal right of inheritance the same as

Harrison's three younger children. At that secret adoption years ago, he'd had no choice but to agree to this, as it was New Jersey law, and the cloak-and-dagger adoption could never have taken place otherwise.

If he had left anything in his will—any insurance, even a dollar —it would have gone to his heirs equally, and we were all his legal heirs now, including me. To exact his final revenge on my mother and realize her biggest fear of being penniless, Harrison had to deny his own children any inheritance, and she said that he did so without hesitation and with his last dying breath.

But that wasn't the end of this never ending story. Never one to be on the losing end of things now it was Mom's turn for payback. In return for this eternal financial comeuppance, my mother may have enacted her own final plan. She arranged a funeral and buried Harrison quickly and quietly, allowing no calling hours for anyone who wanted to pay their respects to this once prominent man. In lieu of a viewing and in his published obituary she asked for monetary donations to be sent to her in care of the newly created Harrison F. English Memorial Fund.

In the end, there are no records and no one remembers the memorial fund ever being established. It's likely that if there were any contributions they may have made their way into a newly created and of course fictitious Elizabeth Stapf Handley English Survival Fund. Could the records of any such fund or donations have been incinerated in the famous bonfire?

Revenge is sweet and there was one more final retaliation to go. Mom never allowed a tombstone to be placed on Harrison's grave. She made it very difficult and almost impossible for any visitor to find Harrison's final resting place to pay their last respects. Despite the offers and insistence from Harrison's family to pay for a headstone, she never relented, right up until her death. It was one last screw to turn on Harrison for cancelling his insurance. Fortunately for Harrison, his three children, my half brothers and sister, had a double tombstone installed for both of them to share several years after her passing. Elizabeth no longer had the power to stop it and Harrison got his final recognition.

She was, after all, slicker and craftier than the Ivy League educated Harrison Force English. That may explain the brand new baby blue Jaguar XJ6 with the walnut wood dashboard that she purchased with cash just a few months after the funeral and at the time I was homeless. She proudly drove the luxurious and opulent Jag around Trenton for the rest of her days. It is one of the official cars of the royal families and UK Prime Minister and of course nothing else would do for the Queen of the Manor.

CHAPTER TWENTY

CONCLUSION

Over the next fifteen years, my father Vernon and I grew wonderfully close. I visited Oklahoma as often as I could, with my family or whenever I was traveling on business and could get there. I was headed to visit Dad just before his death on a day America can never and will never forget, September 11, 2001.

I was traveling on business, and I was at the airport in Dallas, Texas. I had booked a short flight into Oklahoma City, and Dad and I were going to have what would have been our last father/son reunion.

As I was boarding the plane in Dallas, terrorists hijacked four airliners, and three of them hit the World Trade Center and the Pentagon. Thanks to the brave passengers, the fourth crashed in a field in Pennsylvania, missing its target.

I called my dad, a proud American veteran, and he was crying. He was sick and weak at the time, but he wanted to go fight for his country. He could hardly speak as the events of the day unfolded, so our telephone call was a short one. I said, "Dad, I love you very much and want to come see you, but I need to get back home to my family and make sure they are all right." Dad told me he understood and to be careful. Then we both ended the call by declaring our eternal love for each other.

A friend with me at my business conference had rented a car the day before, and we jumped in and drove nonstop for twenty-two hours to New Jersey and our families. It was a day and night I'll never forget.

I did most of the driving, as I wasn't afraid to push it at ninety-plus miles per hour while my friend slept. All I kept thinking was what the heck was going on with our country? The radio was all I had to keep me posted, and the news was incomplete and sporadic at best. I kept thinking of my father, sick and crying and brokenhearted once again, but this time over our country. We drove the southern route from Dallas that took us within view of the Pentagon, which was still smoldering from the plane crash, and then north to Newark Airport, where we could see the ruins of the World Trade Center still smoking as well. It was horrible seeing both of the terrorists' targets just hours after the attacks.

The next time I saw Dad, it was at his funeral.

I'd never seen a military funeral, and it's quite a moving sight. American flags were everywhere. Eight soldiers from the nearby Ft. Sill Color Guard stood at attention in their finest formal dress, solemn looks on their faces. An American flag was draped over the coffin. Here I was, wondering how I deserved to be a pallbearer for this distinguished soldier and true American hero.

The drums were softly playing in muffled beats. We all walked slowly in perfect step, carrying the coffin from the hearse to its final resting place. There was a service and a prayer. A preacher who knew this man and his family spoke reverently about his life. The sermon was about a good man, a family man and soldier who had dedicated his life to his family and to his country.

Seven of the armed soldiers marched slowly to the gravesite in perfect cadence. They stood in a straight formation while aiming their rifles into the air over the coffin. The eighth soldier called out the order: "Prepare to fire... fire, prepare to fire... fire, prepare to fire... fire." A twenty-one gun salute. A salute to a man who had spent his lifetime both in and out of harm's way protecting the country he loved.

Even President George W. Bush sent a certificate in honor of Vernon Handley, awarded by a grateful nation in recognition of his devotion and consecration to the service of our country.

Vernon Lee Handley was a forgiving man. I would not have been so forgiving. This was a salute and a tribute to an amazing man who had a tremendous impact on my life, although I only knew him for a short period of time.

He served in the US Army for more than thirty years, rising to the rank of command sergeant major. He served in World War II and served two tours of duty in Korea, and then two more in Vietnam. Over his distinguished military career, he was stationed all over the world and spent several years in Germany. Those were the years that unfortunately changed his life forever—our lives forever.

Through thirty years of military service to America, he never complained, except about those who didn't honor the military. He had an aversion to them, and he wasn't shy about saying so. He never told his family what it was like in Korea or in Vietnam. He just couldn't bring himself to talk about it, especially what happened in Vietnam. He served his country as most good soldiers do, honorably and with distinction.

I stood at his grave sobbing. My brain bubbled over with thoughts. I was reeling, drifting back and forth in time, reminiscing about scenes from my childhood to present day. In my head, virtual pictures were being snapped like a PowerPoint presentation of my life.

This same phenomenon had happened to me only once before in my life, many years ago. It happened at the moment I learned that this man, Vernon Lee Handley, existed, as I held my adoption papers in my hand for the first time. Now it was happening to me again as I say our final goodbye.

I thought back to the night of Harrison's death and how mad I was that he hadn't lived long enough for me to punch him in the mouth for all he had done to me over the years. Now I wanted to hurt him again, this time for all he did to my father. I distinctly remember my lack of sorrow about Harrison's death even though at the time I'd thought he was my father. I recalled that horrible realization that there was something mentally wrong with me because I didn't love him. How different it was now to know my real father was gone, and how lucky I was to know the paternal love many of us take for granted. I couldn't fathom the sadness I felt.

I lost my composure when the soldiers marched in and gave him his well-deserved twenty-one gun salute. I was so moved by the ceremony that without knowing why, I walked to one of the soldiers who was picking the twenty-one empty bullet shells off the ground and respectfully asked, "Sir, do you have to account for those empty shells?"

He knew exactly what I was asking for, and he handed me a shell. "No sir, I do not. Here, take this, please." He gently placed the shell into my hand and then he took a step backwards and saluted me. I don't know what came over me, but I just had to possess one of those spent shell casings. Later, everything would make sense to me: why I had asked for the shell, and what I would do with it.

I keep that shell tucked inside of the triangle folded American flag that was flown over the United States Capitol in honor of the Handley family reunion fifteen years before. My stepmother, Rachel, gave me that flag knowing how much it meant to both my father and to me. The shell from his twenty-one gun salute was an added token of the respect the country had for my father.

I had fifteen years with my father, fifteen of the most wonderful years with the most kind and honorable man I have ever met. It should have been a lifetime with him, and it could have been a lifetime, but I can't dwell on what's past. I can only be grateful for what time we had together and the things I learned from Dad in those too-short fifteen years.

And so the soldiers lowered my father's coffin into the ground at that cemetery in Stroud, Oklahoma. As the drums stopped beating and the twenty-one gun salute was finished, all went silent. I shook off the memories and images that flashed through my head, and I began crying while thinking that that little doors on both of our hearts were once again closed and locked, hopefully to be opened again someday at another time and another place.

They were tears of sorrow for the life I could have lived with him. But beyond that, they were tears of joy. A joy that I was lucky enough to know this man for fifteen wonderful years and that I got to learn so much from him. I learned where I came from, who I was, and what made me tick.

Finally, they were tears of great respect for a man who was put through so much in his life, so much more pain and deceit than anyone should ever have to go through. A man robbed of a life with his sons, yet so honorable that he would not dwell on what was past nor say a negative word about anyone, no matter what they did to him.

I learned a lot from my dad. I learned to hug and kiss my children every time I see them because life is short and precious. My children grew up knowing love, and they were not afraid to display it publically.

I've dedicated my life to my children. If the only words etched on my tombstone are, "He was a good father," then my life will have been both successful and complete.

It pleases me that even though I grew up without knowing the love of a father, my children do know that love. Every time they come home, even if it's in front of their friends, I get a hug and a kiss. Since they've become adults, my daughter, Rachael, and my son, Chris, are my best friends forever. They have learned to cherish every minute of life and to live it to the fullest in a positive way and with as good a heart as ever anybody had.

I taught my children that Harrison's old saying that "children should be seen and not heard" was dead wrong. Children should most definitely be heard. They should be heard loud and clear, and most of all, they should be enjoyed. Children and family are the world's most precious gift.

As for my mother, she died a few years later while suffering from dementia. The word "dementia" comes from two Latin words meaning "apart" and "mind," and it is a decline of reasoning, memory and cognitive functions. Dementia is the leading reason that elderly people are placed in institutions such as nursing homes.

In the majority of cases, dementia is incurable. It is a terrible condition that affects both the patient and their loved ones, who have to deal with caring for a parent who might not recognize them.

My mother's dementia progressed until she became totally dependent on others for care. She had an almost complete loss of short-term and long-term memory and was unable to recognize even close relatives as she regressed into a childlike state of mind.

At the end of her life, my mother thought she was living in Germany as a little girl. My sister, who was Mom's best caregiver, would visit her in the nursing home and had to re-introduce herself every day. Mom would tell stories about the people she thought she'd just been speaking to and about the conversations she was having with them. Those people all had died many years before.

As a young girl Elizabeth had spent her years plotting to get herself out of post war Germany at any cost, only to spend her last few months of her life right back where it all started. She was mentally transported back to pre-war Germany, only this time around she was a happy little girl surrounded by her friends and loving family... as it should have been all along.

BLACK ❀ ROSE
writing™

CPSIA information can be obtained
at www.ICGtesting.com
Printed in the USA
FFOW01n1354120515
13251FF